The Value of the Novel

Peter Boxall's *The Value of the Novel* offers a reappraisal of the ethical, political and literary value of the novel as a form at a turning point in the history both of literature and of criticism. As the dominant critical concerns of the twentieth century faded and new cultural and technological environments emerged, Boxall argues that we lost our collective sense of the purpose of the novel. This book responds to this predicament by demonstrating why and how the novel matters to us today. Ranging from Daniel Defoe to Zadie Smith, Boxall shows how the formal properties of the novel allow us to imagine the worlds in which we live. This is a vibrant, compelling and richly informed critical perspective that asks us to see anew how central fiction is to our idea of the world, and how richly the novel informs our attempts to understand our present and our future.

Peter Boxall is Professor of English at the University of Sussex. His books include *Don DeLillo: The Possibility of Fiction*, *Since Beckett: Contemporary Writing in the Wake of Modernism* and *Twenty-First-Century Fiction: A Critical Introduction* (Cambridge University Press, 2013). He has also edited and coedited a number of collections, including *Thinking Poetry* and *1001 Books*.

The Value of the Novel

Peter Boxall
University of Sussex

CAMBRIDGE
UNIVERSITY PRESS

CAMBRIDGE
UNIVERSITY PRESS

University Printing House, Cambridge CB2 8BS, United Kingdom

One Liberty Plaza, 20th Floor, New York, NY 10006, USA

477 Williamstown Road, Port Melbourne, VIC 3207, Australia

314-321, 3rd Floor, Plot 3, Splendor Forum, Jasola District Centre, New Delhi - 110025, India

79 Anson Road, #06-04/06, Singapore 079906

Cambridge University Press is part of the University of Cambridge.

It furthers the University's mission by disseminating knowledge in the pursuit of education, learning and research at the highest international levels of excellence.

www.cambridge.org
Information on this title: www.cambridge.org/9781107637245

First published 2015

A catalogue record for this publication is available from the British Library

ISBN 978-1-107-05749-4 Hardback
ISBN 978-1-107-63724-5 Paperback

Cambridge University Press has no responsibility for the persistence or accuracy of URLs for external or third-party internet websites referred to in this publication, and does not guarantee that any content on such websites is, or will remain, accurate or appropriate.

For Rachael, Susie, William and Georgina

The novel lies, in saying something happened, that did not. It must, therefore, contain uncontradictable truth to warrant the original lie.

Elizabeth Bowen, 'Notes on Writing a Novel'

Contents

Acknowledgements

All books are works of collaboration, but this one is perhaps particularly so. There are many people who have been almost as instrumental in the writing of what follows as I have been. My first debt of gratitude is to Ray Ryan, who had the idea for this series, and whose enthusiasm for the novel has been a constant source of inspiration. Without his invitation, I would not have written this book, and so never have learnt the lessons about the value of fiction that writing it has taught me. But many others too have shaped what follows. More than any other book I have written, this one owes a debt to the students I have worked with over the years I have been teaching at the University of Sussex. There is no better way to learn about the novel than to talk about it in a seminar room, and every sentence of this book has its origin, in part, in that most utopian of spaces. Friends and colleagues, too numerous to name here, have had a hand, too, in every line. But my warmest thanks go to my family. My partner Hannah is the reader I have in my head, and her opinion, real or imagined, colours everything I write. My children are their own bildungsroman, kunstlerroman, comedy, science fiction and avant-garde. This book is dedicated to my brother and sisters. We grew up together reading novels, for which we all still have a passion. Perhaps living in a busy house meant that we turned to fiction for solitude. But one of the values of the novel is that it allows us to be alone and in company at the same time. Reading fiction for me, even now, evokes this mixture of solitude and company, and always carries an echo of my shared childhood with them.

Introduction: The Value of the Novel

> The ceaseless pursuit of data to quantify the value of any endeavour is catastrophic to true understanding.
>
> Dave Eggers, *The Circle*[1]

We are living now at a critical time in the history of our collective understanding of value. Across cultures, in a number of different, interlocking ways, and at local and international levels, one can see fundamental shifts occurring in the processes by which cultural value is produced and disseminated.

The first of these shifts has to do with the fate of what, in the humanities over the last half century, has been called 'theory'. Somewhere in the middle of the last century our understanding of the role and the purpose of the humanities underwent a revolution, sparked by the emergence of 'theory' as a new critical discourse, which turned many of the assumptions that had driven our response to the arts on their head. Where the spokespersons for the arts in the earlier half of the century saw the humanities as the guardian of a set of (western) cultural values, a new generation of critics that came to prominence in the sixties and seventies (including figures such as Jacques Derrida, Roland Barthes, Michel Foucault and Julia Kristeva) developed a much more critical and sceptical approach to the very concept of value itself. For these later critics, the role of art was not to uphold any particular ideology or any given cultural, ethical or moral doctrine or creed; on the contrary, art and literature were valuable precisely insofar as they were able to set value aside. It was the freedom of the critical imagination from ideological prescription, from any compulsory adherence to commonly held 'values', that granted the arts their extraordinary power. Where influential critics in the earlier decades of the century, such as F.R Leavis, Q.D. Leavis and I.A. Richards, assigned to the arts a moral purpose, charging newly defined university departments in the humanities with the task of preserving a set of cultural values from the perceived threat of decline, the explosion of revolutionary thinking in the 1960s and 1970s drew its energy from a furious rejection of this conservatism. It was the arts which were able, uniquely, to give expression to new cultural possibilities, to decolonise the mind, to loosen the grip of the patriarchal, the heteronormative and the rational in order to explore the nonnormative, the transgressive, the dissident; and it was in part the concerted attack on 'value', the overturning of prior conceptions of cultural propriety, that enabled this revolution to take place.

If this struggle between the Leavisites and the new wave of critics committed to 'theory' determined the course of the humanities through the last decades of the twentieth century, however, the first decades of the new century have seen something like a reversal in our conception of value. The 'theory wars', as the struggle was known in the eighties and nineties, were well and truly won by the theorists, and the revolutionary thinking made possible by Derrida, Barthes and Foucault became a new kind of orthodoxy. But with the apparent triumph of theory, and with the reshaping of the humanities that came in its wake, we have seen a curious depletion in the energy that drove the theory wars themselves, and with it a creeping nostalgia for the old spectres of cultural value that had seemed so effectively to have been vanquished. As we move into what has been called a 'post-theory' era, we have seen, across a wide range of cultural fora, the growing desire for a new means of articulating a set of values for our own generation, of staging what Dorothy J. Hale has called a 'new ethical defense of literary value'.[2]

To chart this volte face in one of its many incarnations, one only has to look at the trajectory taken by the career of Terry Eagleton, one of the most prominent Marxist literary critics of his generation.[3] Eagleton's 1983 work *Literary Theory: An Introduction* marks a critical moment in the establishment of 'theory' as an orthodoxy. This was a work that gave one of the most influential accounts of theory as the privileged prism through which literature should be read – and was one of the first to introduce undergraduates en masse to theory as a foundation of literary thinking. And central to this 'introduction' is the rejection of literary value as a guiding concept. In the opening chapter of the book, entitled 'What Is Literature', Eagleton carefully explains that 'anything can be literature', and conversely that 'anything which is regarded as unalterably and unquestionably literature – Shakespeare for example – can cease to be literature'.[4] To read literature critically, one has to develop a critical understanding of what Eagleton later called the 'ideology of the aesthetic',[5] to develop a thoroughly sceptical attitude to the 'institution' called literature – even to the extent, Eagleton says, that 'when I use the words "literary" and "literature" from here on in this book, I place them under an invisible crossing-out mark' (p. 9). To read 'theoretically', he suggests, is to recognise, contra ideologues such as Q.D. Leavis and I.A. Richards, that 'there is no such thing as a literary work or tradition which is valuable *in itself*, regardless of what anyone might have said or come to say about it' (p. 10). It is only when we recognise this, when we see that '"Value" is a transitive term' that 'means whatever is valued by certain people in specific situations, according to particular criteria and in the light of given purposes' (p. 10), that we can read literature as a *critique* of ideological forces, rather than simply a product of them. Everything that Eagleton goes on to say about theory – in his subsequent trawl through structuralism, poststructuralism and psychoanalysis – follows from this initial act of demystification, this rejection of the principle that literature enshrines value. But thirty years later, in his 2013 book *How to Read Literature*, Eagleton seems to have turned full circle and comes to endorse the principle of literary value – as an antidote to perceived cultural decline – fully as enthusiastically as Leavis and Richards. This later Eagleton, very like Richards in his 1924 work *The Principles of Literary Criticism*, fears that we no longer know how to read literature, that 'like clog dancing, the art of analysing works of literature is almost dead on its feet'.[6] It is no longer our duty to cast doubt on the intrinsic value of literature; rather, our urgent task now, in the wake of theory, is to remind ourselves what literature is, and how to read it, by 'paying close attention to literary form and technique' (p. ix). The liberating idea, so central to *Literary Theory*, that 'anything can be literature', is now, for Eagleton, the tiresome confusion that has to be resolved. Readers today tend to 'set aside the "literariness"' of what they read, and so are unable to appreciate the distinction between 'a poem or play or novel', and 'an account of the incidence of soil erosion in Nebraska'. 'It is true', Eagleton admits,

> that one could always read a report on soil erosion in this 'literary' way. It would simply mean paying close attention to the workings of its language. For some literary theorists, this would be enough to turn it into a work of literature, though probably not one to rival *King Lear*. (pp. 2–3)

Where the 1983 Eagleton is keen to imagine a time when Shakespeare might be drained of literary value, a time when 'Shakespeare would be no more valuable than much present day graffiti' (p. 10), the Eagleton of 2013 holds Shakespeare as an example of literary value that not even the most extreme example of bad reading can challenge. In 1983 the task was to strip reading of pre-existing value judgements; in 2013 it is to find a way of rediscovering precisely these values, as a means of re-educating the public on how to read. Literary works, the 2013 Eagleton writes, 'demand a particularly vigilant kind of reading, one which is alert to tone, mood, pace, genre, syntax, grammar, texture, rhythm, narrative structure, punctuation, ambiguity – in fact to everything that comes under the heading of form' (p. 2). It is these critical principles that we must attend to now, rather than any Marxist debunking of aesthetic ideology, because if we don't the very thing that we are setting out to theorise – literature itself – might melt into air, too effectively neutralised by those 'invisible crossing-out marks' that Eagleton wielded so enthusiastically in the midst of his revolutionary zeal.

This reversal, of course, is a very localised one, to be explained as much by the passage of Eagleton's thinking as by any larger reassertion of value. But nevertheless, the trajectory taken by Eagleton's work does accord with a more general sense that the 'literary' itself, so long repressed by literary theorists as a dubious term laden with ideological baggage, is starting to return. Not only is there a wave of criticism – by a wide and very diverse range of critics such as Dorothy

Hale, Martha Nussbaum, Joshua Landy, Lisa Zunshine, Sianne Ngai, Helen Small, Liam McIlvanney and Ray Ryan, among others[7] – which sets out to reinvent a critical vocabulary with which to address literary value, but the teaching of literature in the academy itself is undergoing a significant reorganisation. While 'theory' was the dominant force in the Anglo-American academy through the final decades of the last century, the new century has seen an accelerated shift away from 'theory' and towards 'creative writing' as the engine which drives literary thinking. As Mark McGurl demonstrated in his influential book *The Program Era*, the growth of creative writing programmes in the United States throughout the postwar decades has become exponential in recent years, as academia has increasingly set the terms not only of how literature is read, but also of how it is produced.[8] Where 'theory' bred a generation of critics who were sceptical of the validity of literature itself as an object of study, the 'program era' is tilting us in the other direction, towards a situation in which the distinction between creative and critical writing is becoming more difficult to sustain, and in which critical writing itself is becoming increasingly 'literary', increasingly belle-lettristic. Where the last generation practised a thoroughgoing scepticism about the validity of literature as an object of study, the current generation is growing up with a scepticism about the possibility of criticism as an autonomous activity. To address literature now, one is encouraged to produce it, to exercise one's 'creativity' – like the clones in Kazuo Ishiguro's novel *Never Let Me Go* – rather than one's critical faculties.

Alongside this shift from theory towards creative writing – from theory to practice – as the guiding principle of critical thought in the academy, we have seen a much larger, more systemic instrumentalisation of the academy itself – an instrumentalisation which is bound up with the renewed emphasis on value as the operative term in critical analysis. If literary critics are finding themselves now reasserting the value of their discipline, so universities throughout the English-speaking world are forced, by ever more stringent forms of government control, to produce evidence of the value of their own modes of inquiry. While the era of high theory in Anglophone universities had its own kind of instrumentality – driven as it was by the perceived need to redistribute what John Guillory has called (after Pierre Bourdieu) 'cultural capital' – the contemporary university is coming under increasing pressure to adapt its procedures to the demands, and the logic, of the global market place.[9] In recent years, universities across the developed world have undergone some version of what David Lurie, in J.M. Coetzee's 1999 novel *Disgrace*, calls the 'great rationalization'. 'Once a professor of modern languages' at Cape Town University College, Lurie says that, since 'Classics and Modern Languages were closed down', he has been an 'adjunct professor of communications'.[10] 'Like all rationalized personnel', he goes on, Lurie is allowed to teach one course a year on his own specialisation – in this case, romantic poetry – but for the rest of the time 'he teaches Communications 101, "Communication Skills", and Communication 201, "Advanced Communication skills"' (p. 3). This reorganisation, he says, is undertaken in order to put literary knowledge to some kind of practical socioeconomic use. The 'first premise' of 'his new discipline', as 'enunciated in the Communications 101 handbook', is that 'Human society has created language in order that we may communicate our thoughts, feelings and intentions to each other' (pp. 3–4). Anyone working in a literature department in an English-speaking university in the first decades of the new century will recognise this premise – that literature is not to be valued or understood on its own terms, but as part of a wider cultural, social or economic good. As is boasted in the mission statement of a fictional university in Margaret Atwood's novel *Oryx and Crake*, the aim of the contemporary university is not to open a space for disinterested thought – or for what is now sometimes called, in a rather chilling term, 'blue skies research' – but to teach transferable life skills, to make reading literature the occasion for learning how to be good and productive citizens, who can effectively communicate their intentions to each other. Atwood's university has a high minded motto in Latin, which declares that '*Ars Longa Vita Brevis*', but in case this devotion to the arts might be off-putting to the parents of prospective students, the Latin motto is accompanied by an English one which is both more direct and more practical – 'Our Students Graduate with Employable Skills'.[11]

The contemporary tendency towards a reassertion of literary value – Hale's 'ethical defense' – is, then, bound up with the requirement that universities make themselves 'viable' in the contemporary market place – that, in the terms employed by the UK academy, they demonstrate that their disciplines have verifiable social and economic 'impact'. And, alongside this problematic coupling, the question of value today is determined by a third, even more wide-ranging and systemic development in the production and dissemination of literary knowledge – that is, the emergence of the internet as the new site of public discussion and debate. As Ronan McDonald argues in his important 2007 book *The Death of the Critic*, the spectacular rise of social media has effectively democratised the process of evaluation, meaning that the 'age of the critic as the arbiter for public taste and cultural consumption seems to have passed'.[12] McDonald sees a continuity between the rejection of literary value in the university during the age of theory, and the appearance of the online commentariat – the blogger, the reviewer on Amazon – as a new forum of public criticism. Universities abdicated their role as *evaluators* of culture last century and so now, with the appearance of a vast and uncontainable public sphere in which we are all encouraged to evaluate everything from Chinese takeaways to holiday villas to productions of *King Lear*, the professional literary critic has little or no purchase on the process by which literary value is understood. McDonald's response to this situation is to open another front in that 'defense of literary value' staged by Hale, and to urge the humanities to return to their primary task of evaluating, of weighing and judging the value of literature, thus setting the terms of the public debate again. If, in the best case scenario, the critic is not dead but simply in a deep coma, McDonald argues, the 'first step in reviving him or her is to bring the idea of artistic merit back to the heart of academic criticism' (p. 149). 'If criticism is to be valued', he suggests, 'if it is to reach a wide public, it needs to be evaluative' (p. 149). Dave Eggers' 2013 novel *The Circle* offers a stark picture of the fate of the critic, and of the university, if the logic of communal life inherent in the rise of Google is to go unchecked. In Eggers' novel, it is the headquarters of the global media company *The Circle* (a loose fictionalisation of Google) that offers itself as 'the campus', and the task of evaluation – not only of the arts but of all forms of public, political and democratic life – has passed to 'the people', through the hands of the giant and all powerful corporation. In this nightmare version of the rise of the public critic, all citizens evaluate and judge at all moments of every day, but of course, with the complete democratisation of the public sphere, with what is imagined as complete 'transparency', comes an utter failure of the critical faculty, a loss of those forms of privacy and critical distance that are essential, in Eggers' terms, to 'true understanding' (p. 485).

It is in the context of these mutations in our understanding of value that this book sets out to rethink the value of the novel. To ask what the value of the novel is today – to seek to reassess and redefine why we read novels, and what they are for – is to engage this set of often contradictory imperatives. It is to join a group of thinkers who see that now, in the wake of the theoretical developments of the last century, and with the decline of postmodernism as a cultural dominant, it becomes not only timely but also necessary to produce a new means of understanding what kind of a thing literature is – how it differs from other forms of representation, how it makes meaning, how literary form allows us to imagine and represent the cultures in which we live. As the energy that drove the theoretical terms in which these questions were couched in recent decades has dwindled, we enter into a transitional period in the history of both literature and criticism in which it is necessary to pose them once again, to rethink the paradigms and the cultural forms in which we frame our sense of literary value, our sense of why and how literature matters. The revolutionary literary thinking that flourished in the second half of the last century harnessed the earlier discoveries of Darwin, Marx and Freud to produce a truly transformative understanding of the world-making potential of the arts; but if the legacy of that revolution is to extend meaningfully into the new century – and into what has (somewhat regrettably) been called the post-postmodern moment – we now need to develop a new set of critical languages with which to articulate the enduring power of literature and the arts to invent for us an idea of the world, to 'shape', as one of Don DeLillo's narrators puts it, 'the way we think and see'.[13] But if the legacy of 'theory' pushes us in this direction, the danger is that, in doing so, we are led also, as Eagleton was in 2013, to cancel that very scepticism about the ideology of value that drove theory in the first place. To enter now into the discourse of value is to risk aligning oneself with those forces that are 'rationalising' the university, that are requiring the humanities to 'account' for themselves, to make claims about their social and economic value that are comically at odds with their own disinterestedness, their own critical detachment from the commodity, the market place, the whole question, indeed, of value. The challenge that faces those who would measure, now, the value of the arts, is how to capture and articulate the ethical force of the literary, without resurrecting a conservative, Leavisite critical language in which to express it; how to produce an adequately rich account of the democratic power of the literary imagination, its capacity to continually remake the world in which we live, without returning to a prior model of the critic as 'arbiter of public taste'; how to inherit the legacy of theory, without betraying its spirit.

Indeed, the attempt to bring the language of value to the novel now might risk a kind of rebuff from the fictions themselves, from novels which are written in the teeth of a contemporary culture which ruthlessly commodifies the author, relentlessly driving him or her to adopt a persona and a genre which can be readily marketed and monetised. Coetzee's David Lurie makes a typically melancholic, muted complaint against the forces which marshal both critic and novelist into communication when he quietly but rather devastatingly rejects the terms of his own courses, 'Communications 101 and 102': 'Although he devotes hours of each day to his new discipline', he says, he finds its premise, that humans create language to communicate with one another, 'preposterous'. 'His own opinion', he goes on, 'which he does not air, is that the origins of speech lie in song, and the origins of song in the need to fill out with sound the overlarge and rather empty human soul' (p. 4). Lurie, and perhaps Coetzee, chooses a kind of empty sound over the requirement that language should be briskly effective, fit for purpose. And if Coetzee's response to this requirement is a typical blend of the stately and the melancholic, then Philip Roth's is typically intemperate, furious, scattershot: 'There was a time', the deranged critic Amy Bellette writes in Roth's 2007 novel *Exit Ghost*, 'when intelligent people used literature to think'; but, she goes on, 'that time is coming to an end'.[14] The culture of accountability, the culture of the rationalised university, forces literature into a utilitarianism which means that it can no longer help one to think, can only imprison one more narrowly in the way things are. 'The predominant uses to which literature is now put', Bellette writes with growing fury,

> in the culture pages of the enlightened newspapers and in university English departments are so destructively at odds with the aims of imaginative writing, as well as with the rewards that literature offers an open-minded reader, that it would be better if literature were no longer put to any public use. (p. 182)

If one sets out to judge the novel, to put it to good use, to ask how it might serve an ethical function or have a cultural value, one might find oneself incurring the wrath of Roth, or the lofty disdain of Coetzee. The novel now has, and perhaps has always had, a streak of steely resistance to those who would evaluate it – to its readers, who one of Samuel Beckett's narrators refers to, at a memorable moment, as 'cunts like you'.[15] But if the process of reading, of evaluating, risks encountering this kind of resistance, this is absolutely not a reason to stop pushing at the novel, to stop asking why and how it matters, in the full expectation of a satisfactory answer. Indeed, it is a central premise of this book that the novel's particular resistance to reading, its perennial refusal of the conventions within which we might seek to evaluate it, is one of its greatest gifts, and a source of its own ethical thinking, its uniquely powerful capacity to critique the cultures from which it emerges and within which it is read. This is not of course to deny that the novel has a positive cultural function, or that it offers itself to readers as a means of imagining modes of collective life. The novel, more than any other art form or mode of representation, has provided, since its emergence in its modern form in the eighteenth century, the forms with which we have fashioned our cultural communities.[16] However 'preposterous' it might seem, to Lurie, to suggest that literature might have some kind of social function – might help us to 'communicate our thoughts, feelings and intentions to each other' – it is the novel that has allowed us to narrate to ourselves the passage of modern democracy, the novel that has given us the closest and most intimate access to the minds of others, so that we might build collective life-worlds. As Nancy Armstrong has recently put it, 'the history of the novel and the history of the modern subject are, quite literally, one and the same'.[17] But, and this is central to everything I will be arguing in this book, the world-making power of prose fiction arises from the capacity of the novel to reject or suspend the forms of community that it helps to create. The resistance to evaluation that we find in Roth, in Beckett and Coetzee, this is not some late denial of the cultural role of the novel, but the very fuel that has driven the novel's long exercise in world-making. The novel, in proposing a narrative form for common experience, has always, since its inception, exercised a kind of freedom from the conventions that it articulates, a kind of freedom that is woven into its status as fiction, its immunity from anything like responsibility to existing truth. It is written into the genetics of the novel form that it should exceed the conventions which it enables, that it should remain in some sense unreadable, in some sense ahead of the culture in which it is written and received. This is why Coetzee's Lurie finds the university's commitment to enforced communication so preposterous; this is what inspires Amy Bellette's crazed desire to 'forbid all public discussion of literature in newspapers, magazines and scholarly periodicals', to 'forbid all instruction in literature in every grade school, high school, college, and university in the country' (p. 184). If we are to understand the value of the novel, its capacity to make the worlds in which we live, then we have also to understand its resistance to value as presently understood or constituted, its *right* to be judged not by the terms that we have available, but by those futural forms which it alone is able to summon into existence. If we are to capture now what McIlvanney and Ryan call the 'novelness' of the novel, we need to respond, as they put it, to its 'distinctive kind of ontology', which is based not on a commitment to an existing set of values, but on an originary 'uncertainty' which draws its truths from its encounter with the 'partial' and the 'provisional'.[18]

It is this gift that the novel has – to represent our shared communities and to suspend the ties that bind them – that this book seeks to address, at a time when our own critical and cultural communities are undergoing a period of profound change. In order to approach this double movement – in which the novel both shapes the world and resists its demands – what follows is broken into two parts, entitled 'Art' and 'Matter'. These parts take their name from Shakespeare's *Hamlet* – from that moment when Gertrude tells the pompous Polonius that his windy rhetorical speeches should contain 'more matter', and 'less art' (2.2.97). The distinction that Gertrude makes here between art and matter – a distinction which is central, I think, to *Hamlet* – is crucial to any discussion of literary value. If we are to imagine that art has a value, a purpose, then we are led to imagine also that the artwork, defined by its formal features, has some kind of relationship to the world which simply is, to Gertrude's 'matter', a relationship in which the artwork is answerable to that world, and comes after it. The artwork is judged by its capacity to represent the world truly, to find a form in which to give expression to a pre-existing set of realities. The chapters of this book are organised, accordingly, around this distinction between form and content. Part I, 'Art', focuses on the formal procedures by which the novel has crafted its communities. Chapter 1, 'The Novel Voice' offers a reassessment of the capacity of narrative voice to speak to us directly and inwardly, like a parent reading to a child, and in so doing asks how this intimate address allows the novel to conjure a uniquely vivid experience of presence. Chapter 2, 'Is This Really Realism?', gives an account of the development of realism, from Defoe to Kafka, in order to examine the particular means by which the novel has made pictures of the world. Part II, 'Matter', offers an account of how these formal properties allow the novel to make and furnish homes for ourselves in the world. The three chapters of this part focus first on how the novel imagines bodies in space, then on how narrative situates bodies in the flow of time and lastly on how the novel helps us to produce a critical understanding of the law, as it operates upon bodies in space and in time.

In offering this schematic account of the novel, from across its modern history, this book presents a concentrated snapshot of the means by which the novel has fashioned the narratives in which we encounter the world. But if the distinction between Part I and Part II – between 'Art' and 'Matter' – helps us to describe the novel in this way, allowing us to make a critical picture of how the novel form has worked on and in the world, what this book argues throughout is that art and matter, form and content, are intimately related to the point that the separation between them is continually disappearing. It may be that the distinction between form and content is crucial to our understanding of all works of art, that without it we cannot maintain a working distinction between the real and the imaginary, between the material and the ideal. It may be, also, that we cannot imagine a means of evaluating the work, of according it an ethics or a politics, without sustaining this difference between the world as it is and the world as we picture it in aesthetic forms. But what this book discovers, at every turn, is that it is the particular gift of the novel to overcome this distinction, to demonstrate repeatedly how art is always becoming matter, and how matter is always becoming art. As Martha Nussbaum puts it, 'Style itself makes its claims, expresses its own sense of what matters.'[19] If the novel matters today, if it has a value, then it is because it has this unique ability to put the relationship between art and matter, between words and the world, into a kind of motion, to work at the disappearing threshold between the world that exists and that which does not, between the world that we already know and understand and that which we have not yet encountered.

Indeed, it is this particular ability, this novel gift, that is felt as a critical absence at the heart of *Hamlet* – a play, I think, which is seized with a longing for the kind of intricate interiority that belongs, perhaps, to the modern novel, and that was not yet available for Shakespeare in 1599. 'More matter with less art', Gertrude snaps at Polonius, urging him to get to the point, to simply say what he means. But the central problem of *Hamlet* is that, when the world is in a process of transition, when the 'time is out of joint', the relationship between words and what they mean, between art and matter, becomes uncertain, difficult to rely on. Claudius recognises this gulf between signs and things at work in both his troubled stepson/nephew and his new wife. Meeting Gertrude fresh from her incestuous closet scene with Hamlet, Claudius is clearly annoyed by her panting, lusty disarray. 'There's matter in these sighs', he says pettishly to Gertrude, 'these profound heaves;/ You must translate. 'Tis fit we understand them' (4.1.1–2). And if Gertrude's unspeakable love for her son is a matter that cannot quite come to language, that remains unreadable or untranslatable, so Hamlet's love for his father seems too to resist articulation. Claudius thinks of Hamlet's antic mourning for his father as a

> something-settled matter in his heart,
> Whereon his brains still beating puts him thus
> From fashion of himself. (3.1.175–7)

Love for one's father, love for one's son is, like the time itself, out of joint, and the central struggle of this play, at the dawn of European modernity, is to find a way of putting things back together so that we are no longer alienated from our own self-fashioning, so that the mechanisms of inheritance from one generation to the next might be restored. But if the play struggles to achieve this, if it fails to translate the matter in Gertrude's sighs, the matter that sets Hamlet's brain beating against itself like a confused heart, it secretes within itself the idea of the novel, as a form in which matter and art might come together in a way that they cannot on the renaissance stage. The ghost of Old Hamlet famously implores his son to 'remember me', and Hamlet's impassioned response might be read as the longing for an as yet non-existent form in which to accommodate the memory of his father, to give expression to that 'something-settled matter in his heart'. 'Remember thee', Hamlet cries,

> Yea, from the table of my memory
> I'll wipe away all trivial fond records,
> All saws of books, all forms, all pressures past,
> That youth and observation copied there,

And thy commandment alone shall live
Within the book and volume of my brain
Unmixed with baser matter.   (1.5.98–104)

Neither Hamlet, of course, nor Shakespeare can draw on the
resources of the modern novel to give expression to Hamlet's
love for his father. The 'book and volume' in which the matter
in Hamlet's heart might be translated remains for them imaginary, still to come. But I think it is not too fanciful to suggest that
the book that Hamlet imagines here, the book in which it might
be possible to meet with the mind of another with an intimacy
and intensity that is unmixed with baser matter, is the book that
became known as the novel. *Hamlet* depicts and performs the
emergence of a modern subjectivity, a mode of being and thinking
that did not find ready expression in the forms that Shakespeare
had to hand. In order for this new mode of being to give expression to itself, to fashion itself, we require the novel, with its
heightened sense of interiority, its extraordinary capacity to put
ideas into transformative contact with matter. In tracing the play
between art and matter, as it plays through the history of the
novel from Daniel Defoe to Zadie Smith, this book will suggest
that the novel is perfectly fitted to the expression of the modern
subject, that the novel is able, more fully than any other form, to
give narrative expression to the ways in which we inhabit our
bodies in space and time, under the authority of the law. But it
will also suggest, at a moment in the history of the western
subject that is perhaps as precarious and transformative as that
which gave rise to *Hamlet*, that the novel harbours new ways of
experiencing embodiment, new ways of experiencing space and
time, under an emerging global regime that is almost unreadable
to us. If the novel is valuable now, it is not only because it has
helped us to make a home for ourselves in the world that already
exists, but also because it allows us to imagine and to make new
worlds, to fashion new forms of accommodation between art and
matter, or even to live in a condition of worldlessness. If we are
living at a disjunct time when we are required to rethink our

understanding of value, when we have to adapt our critical languages and institutions to newly emerging global realities, then the novel might help us to achieve this. It is not only, perhaps, that we are required now to think again about how to read the novel, but also that we should ask the novel to read us, to give form to an emergent mode of democracy and of subjectivity that ''tis fit we understand'.

PART I

Art

1 The Novel Voice

If someone speaks, it gets lighter.

Sigmund Freud, *General Theory of the Neuroses*[1]

By the voice a faint light is shed. Dark lightens while it sounds.

Samuel Beckett, *Company*[2]

I

I want to start a discussion of the value of the novel, then, by thinking about the voice in which the novel speaks to us, and I want to ask, more specifically, what the experience of attending to that voice is like – to ask, in effect, what you *hear* when you read. Do you hear what you are reading as a voice in your head? Does the novel speak in a particular kind of voice, a voice specific to its form, which is proper to the novel itself? Is the novel as a form particularly well adapted to creating the conditions of voice and of hearing, to producing a scenario in which a speaker addresses us in what George Eliot has called our 'inward voice'?[3] And does this inward voice talk to us in a particularly intimate way, entangling itself with the voice with which we think, with which we speak to ourselves? As Don DeLillo's narrator puts it, at the shattering opening of his novel *Underworld*, is it the case that the novel 'speaks in your voice', entering into the most private spaces in which you give sound and form to thought and words?[4] Does the value of the novel emerge in some way from its uncanny capacity to animate voice, to capture the rhythms and modulations not only of the voices of others, but of our own voice as it sounds in our head?

These, in a sense, are questions we have trained ourselves not to ask. Ever since Michel Foucault began his famous 1969 lecture 'What Is an Author?' with Samuel Beckett's question, 'What does it matter who is speaking?', we have become accustomed to treating the question of the speaking voice, as it relates to reading and writing, with suspicion.[5] Both Foucault, in 1969, and Roland Barthes, in his equally influential 1968 essay 'The Death of the Author', insist that it does not matter in the least who is speaking. The writing that we attend to as critics and readers of fiction is not linked to some individual speaker, some human bearer of a voice, but is rather to be thought of as a series of dispersed meaning effects, whose dispersal frees us from the illusions and restrictions of embodied being. Foucault insists, in answer to his own Beckettian question, that the 'essential basis' of writing is not the recovery of voice, but its disappearance. Writing, he says, 'is primarily concerned with creating an opening where the writing subject disappears' (p. 116). As Barthes wrote in 1968, it is axiomatic that we 'shall never know' who is speaking, 'for the good reason that writing is the destruction of every voice, every point of origin'.[6] Indeed, it is clear that, for both Barthes and Foucault, the new forms of literary analysis that emerged in the late sixties, and that continue to shape critical thinking today, are based upon our capacity to rid ourselves of the tendency to associate narrative with voice. The long history of humanism, to which the structuralism of Barthes and Foucault sought in part to offer a corrective, has been organised around the primacy of the voice, as the marker of human exceptionalism. In making a fundamental distinction between the speaking subject and the effects of discourse – in insisting that 'voice' is 'not the true place of the writing' (p. 147), that 'writing begins' when 'voice loses its origin' (p. 142) – Barthes and his contemporaries make the uncoupling of voice and narrative the inaugural act of structuralist criticism. It was the task of 'theory', if one can generalise to this extent, to deconstruct what Mladen Dolar calls 'the voice as the source of originary self-presence', to overthrow the myth of voice as 'self-transparency, the hold in presence' that was central to the metaphysical humanist tradition.[7]

So, to raise again the question of the relationship between novel and voice, to ask what we hear when we read, is to set oneself against a critical current that runs at least from the sixties, and to risk re-animating a series of humanist assumptions that we might have thought were long dead. The argument about whether there is or is not a voice in the text has already been had, and the humanists have lost. Andrew Gibson is thus emboldened, in a 2001 essay on voice and narrative, to state categorically that 'there are in fact no narrative voices and no voices in literary narrative, whether the voices of authors, narrators or personae'.[8] Narrative is not the place where someone speaks, but quite definitively the opposite; 'narrative', Gibson writes, 'is the tomb of speech' (p. 643). If there is any persistent or residual belief in the presence of a voice in the text, then this might be understood as the stubborn persistence of a residual humanism that lives on after its own demise. 'Humanists', Gibson writes, 'would find it hard indeed to relinquish the belief that they "hear" a text' (p. 641); so to suggest that the question of voice is something that is still pertinent to us today is to align oneself with that deluded, reactionary rump of critics and readers who can't quite disabuse themselves of metaphysical myth. This indeed is part of Gibson's argument in his 2001 essay. But while Gibson asserts and assumes the absence of voice in literary narrative, what is most striking about his attention to narrative voice is his acknowledgement that, however effectively we have dispensed with it as an aesthetic or narrative category or effect, it nevertheless continues to exert a peculiar hold over the literary imagination. It is not just doddery old humanists that are susceptible to the 'dream of "hearing" the other in the text'; this dream lives on 'even in the most advanced, contemporary, narratological work' (p. 641). It may be the case that narrative is the tomb of speech but, Gibson argues, this does not mean that we have yet learnt fully to accept its silence, or to hear the absence of the voice within it. A question remains, he says, about 'whether it is currently possible to think narrative *without* thinking voice'. 'Do we know', he asks, 'how to attend to the muteness of narrative, how *not* to hear it?' (p. 643).

It is this persistent hearing effect, this voice that lives on after the death of voice, that I want to address here, as it relates to the imperatives of contemporary criticism. I argued earlier that the

critical mood of the first decades of the twenty-first century is domi-
nated by the question of the legacies left to us by the critical movements of the twentieth – that we are led at this 'post-theoretical'
moment to take stock, to assess how a past generation of thinkers
has shaped the critical landscape in which we now live. And as we
enter this period, the question of the voice, and its relation to narrative, once again becomes key. If, as Andrew Gibson suggests, there is
something insistent about the experience of hearing in relation to
reading, if we have struggled to learn 'how *not* to hear' narrative, this
might touch on the way that we receive the legacies of theory. It may
be that this stubborn persistence of voice is simply due to the potency
of humanist myth noted by Barthes – it may be nothing more than a
humanist residue that theory has failed to sublimate. Or, more inter-
estingly, it may be that our understanding of hearing now has to do
with a relationship between speech and writing that has always been
at stake in the novel, that theory has only partially codified, and that
remains compelling as a legacy of theory; a question of the way that
novels make meaning that lies at the heart of critical theory, as it lies
at the heart of the novel itself, and that emerges now into a new kind of
thinkability.

II

In addressing this question here, I am going to discuss two writers,
working at different moments in the history of the novel – writers who
have conventionally been regarded in opposition to one another. I am
going to look at the work of Charles Dickens, particularly his great
novel *David Copperfield*, alongside that of Samuel Beckett, particularly his trilogy of novels written a century later, and the fizzles of
prose that emerged from the 1950s to the very late 1980s. *David
Copperfield* was published in 1850, at a high point in the history of
the novel. Nathaniel Hawthorne published *The Scarlet Letter* in 1850,
Gustave Flaubert began work on *Madame Bovary* in 1850, Elizabeth
Gaskell published *Cranford* in 1851, Herman Melville published
Moby Dick in 1851 and Harriet Beecher Stowe published *Uncle*

Tom's Cabin in 1852. This is a moment in the history of the novel at which the possibilities of realism, the capacity of the novel to depict and fashion a world, were reaching new heights. In contrast, Beckett's writing by many accounts oversees the failure of the modern novel, as fashioned by Defoe and perfected by Austen, Brontë, Flaubert, Dickens, Melville, Tolstoy, Eliot and James. His 1950s trilogy, particularly *Malone Dies*, might be seen as the moment in the postwar period when the fortunes of the novel, transformed as they were by the modernist experiments of Woolf, Joyce, Kafka and Stein, went into a kind of terminal decline. It is in *Malone Dies*, one might suggest, that the very possibility of telling stories expires. In telling the story of Malone – an old man who lies, bedridden and paralysed, trying and failing to write stories as he prepares to die – Beckett is telling the story of the death of storytelling, imagining the death of the imagination. To read Beckett and Dickens together, then, is to compare writers who belong to such different historical moments, and to such different literary traditions, that they might promise to shed little light on each other. But, in suggesting a dialogue between them, one that has eluded most genealogies of the novel, I hope it might be possible to listen for something like a common voice that they share, something that we might think of as a voice that is native to the novel – the voice, perhaps, that we hear when we read.

Of course, any reader of both Beckett and Dickens will recognise at once that, despite their manifest differences, they both worked in the same narrative mode. In three of his most significant novels – *Great Expectations, David Copperfield* and *Bleak House* – Dickens employs a first-person narrative voice (although this is mixed, intriguingly, with present-tense third-person narration in *Bleak House*). Pip, David Copperfield and Esther Summerson are all narrators who write from a vantage point beyond the far horizon of the text, telling the story of their own maturation, the process by which they grow into themselves; and in all three novels the narrative works by drawing attention to the process of observation, remembrance and notation, the process by which the novel itself comes to be written, as a kind of analogue or adjunct to the process by which the narrator him- or herself grows up. Pip, Esther and David all draw attention to their weaknesses: Pip to his snobbish maltreatment of his loving guardian Joe, Esther to her own weakness of understanding concerning the events surrounding her, David to his foolishness, his gullibility, his imperfect understanding of his life as he lives it. As Esther remarks that 'I have not by any means a quick understanding', despite admitting that she can observe things around her closely – that she has 'had always a rather noticing way'[9] – so David repeatedly remarks on the fact that, even as he closely observes the world around him, he doesn't fully understand it as he is in the process of living in it. 'I could observe, in little pieces, as it were', he says of himself as a child, 'but as to making a net of a number of these pieces, and catching anybody in it, that was, as yet, beyond me.'[10] But the reflection back, from a mature vantage point, on the partiality and waywardness of the younger self is what allows the narrator to balance judgement against ignorance, full seeing against partial seeing. Narrating the story of his or her own becoming, these narrators watch their lives, as David puts it, 'rising before my older judgement' (p. 256), allowing the narrative to re-create both the uncertainty of youthful becoming, and the mellow fullness of age. In *David Copperfield*, as in Dickens' other first-person narratives, the story that is told is thus in part that of the process by which the older incarnation brings his or her judgement and experience to bear on the younger, shaping the passage of the protagonist towards his or her own becoming as narrator.

This is a well-recognised narrative mode – what narratologists have come to call homodiegetic or autodiegetic narration. And it is also the mode in which much of Beckett's most significant prose is written, in the period after the war, and with his turn to French language composition. Beckett wrote three stories, in French, in the final months of 1946, which he went on to translate into English as *The Expelled, First Love* and *The Calmative*. It is in these stories that he fashioned the first-person narrative voice in which he wrote *Molloy, Malone Dies* and *The Unnamable*, and which survives in a somewhat altered form in *How It Is*. It is also a version of this voice that continues to recur in Beckett's prose after *How It Is*, although the first-person mood of late works such as *Company* is channelled through a kind of neutral second person. Like Dickens' first-person narratives, all of these works involve the retrospective telling of a story, in which a narrator describes his own becoming in time and his progress towards the place in which he writes the narrative. The narrator of *The Calmative*, for example, describes how he sits down one late evening to 'tell myself a story', which contains the 'myth' of 'another age in which I became what I was';[11] and a version of this scenario is repeated in almost every major prose work that Beckett writes from this point on.

So, both Beckett and Dickens deploy a first-person narrative voice, in order at once to capture in narrative the process of self-becoming, and to reflect critically upon the narrative mechanics of that becoming. But, if this suggests some broad similarities between Beckett's and Dickens' narrative modes, it is of course the case that they use this mode to remarkably different effect. In Dickens' writing, one might argue, the narrative voice is crafted to produce the experience of an extraordinarily powerful *presence*, in which narrator and narrated come together in a fullness of being, one which has its foundations in the magically evocative power of voice itself. This is what Henry James calls, in describing his own spellbound and illicit over-hearing of a recital of *David Copperfield* as a child, Dickens' 'presence and power', which left an 'imprint in the soft clay of our generation', and 'entered into the blood and bone of our intelligence'.[12] The voice in Dickens, as the narrator of *Bleak House* puts it, is so 'rich and mellow', the narrative has such material 'weight', that the 'words' of the text 'really had come to sound as if they had something in them' (p. 576). By contrast, the narrative voice in Beckett's work might appear to tend in the opposite direction – not towards the recuperation of a kind of clayish presence that is proof against the corrosive effects of time, but towards the evacuation of presence, the dismantlement of the myth of the self-identical subject. Take, for example, the opening of the first novel of the trilogy, *Molloy*: 'I am in my mother's room. It's I who live there now'.[13] This opening follows the pattern I have been describing, in which a first-person narrator occupies the scene of narration (here, the mother's room) in the present tense, and tells the story of himself as a character in the past. It is in this room that Molloy writes the narrative that describes his struggle to reach his mother, to make his difficult way to the room in which he finally comes to write the narrative. But even here in the opening breath of *Molloy*, one can see that something has gone wrong with this schema. There is something immediately odd about Molloy's failure to own the room in which he writes. If Molloy now lives in his mother's room, if he has in effect taken her place, then should it not be more properly described as *his* room? And if this makes Molloy's occupation of the room seem strangely partial or out of joint, then of course the use of the word 'there' – 'It's I who live *there* now' – only compounds this sense that Molloy is in some sense absent from the scene of his own dwelling. Molloy is in his mother's room 'now', it is in this room that he writes the narrative, as David Copperfield occupies his own homely room in the narrative present as his story draws to a cadent close, remarking in his final paragraph that 'my lamp burns low, and I have written far into the night' (p. 882). But the 'now' of *Molloy* takes place at a peculiar distance; the room in which the writing takes place is shifted from 'here' to 'there', as the relationship between the incarnations of self in the text – the I that tells the story, and the I that wanders in search of the mother – become confused. Even as we set out, the process of self-capture that animates Dickens' first-person novels, that sets the first person on a journey to himself, becomes skewed, as the narrating I abdicates his fatherly role, refusing to offer a settled here and now, a narrative home, to the character in whose name he speaks. And as we move to the second half of *Molloy*, which is narrated in the first person by another persona named Moran, a private detective of some kind who has apparently been charged with tracking Molloy down, this effect becomes much more drastic. The first lines of Moran's narrative, like those of Molloy's, prepare the narrator for a kind of violent evacuation of self. The opening itself might seem unremarkable on first reading; like many of Beckett's narratives, it simply sets the scene in which Moran writes his story, or what he calls his 'report'. 'It is midnight', he writes. 'The rain is beating on the windows... I get up and go to my desk ... My lamp sheds a soft and steady light' (p. 92). If this paints a homely picture of the scene of narration, however, one that might recall the image of the elderly David Copperfield writing into the night at his lamp-lit desk, the close of the narrative blankly cancels this effect, casting the narrative out of the shelter of its own architecture, its own dwelling place. 'I went back into the house', Moran says at the end of his narrative – after his exhausting attempts to find Molloy have failed, and at that critical, cleft moment at which we are trained to expect the reunion of narrator with narrated self – 'I went back in to the house and wrote, It is midnight. The rain is beating on the windows. It was not midnight. It was not raining' (p. 176). The moment of cleft conjunction becomes, instead, as J.M. Coetzee puts it in another context, a '"decisive moment" of rupture when the past fails to run smoothly into the present".[14]

It is perhaps this catastrophic failure in *Molloy* of the narrator–narrated schema that has led some readers to conclude that Beckett's writing marks a shift in the way that narrative voice functions – a shift in the very texture and timbre of the novel voice itself. Monika Fludernik, for example, suggests that there is a trajectory that we can trace in the history of the novel that takes us gradually away from the 'realistic' and illusionistic devices which give us the impression that we can hear a voice in the text that speaks to us, and towards a recognition that text is in fact made of language, not voices. *David Copperfield*, Fludernik writes, is a classic example of 'natural' narration, in which the narrator replicates a 'real-life schema' where the 'narrative engages in a pretense of authentic autobiography'.[15] With the historical passage from realist to modernist fiction, however, Fludernik suggests that this schema becomes eroded. 'Those modernist texts', she says, 'who present us with the very subjective world of a protagonist through whose consciousness the narrative is focalised', are manifestly 'different from real life' (p. 623) and abandon the pretence that the narrative captures an autobiographical voice that addresses us directly. The passage from realism to modernism and beyond is one that helps us to realise that the voice has always been a fantasy, in which we need no longer believe. 'The text', she says, 'is not a tape recording'; 'attributions of voice', she goes on, are 'realistic or illusionistic interpretive moves' that 'start to flounder' as we move from George Eliot to Henry James, and eventually 'run aground' as we shift from realism to modernism, when 'the usefulness of the narratological concept of voice is exhausted' (p. 635). For the novelist Christine Brooke-Rose, this moment can be rather precisely located (somewhat late in the history of modernism) at the opening of Beckett's novel *Molloy*. It is with Beckett's adoption in *Molloy* of a first-person present tense, she says, that what she calls the 'old regime' of realistic narration was subjected to a kind of coup, an assault in which Beckett was flanked by the newly assembled powers of the *nouveau roman*. Where 'nineteenth-century fiction' shaped first-person narration by casting the narrator in the present tense and the narrated in the past, Beckett's adoption of a peculiarly evacuated present tense, which blurs the distinction between narrator and narrated, between 'here' and 'there', produces just that failure of vocal presence remarked on by Fludernik, and presents readers, Brooke-Rose writes, with the 'astonishing' prospect of an 'I-narrator' who was 'so empty, so "absent from himself"'.[16] This understanding of the passage from realism to modernism, from the nineteenth to the twentieth centuries, suggests that fiction over this period went through a kind of demystification and staged a revelation of the mechanics of its own mimicry of vocal presence. If the second half of the twentieth century saw the emergence of a new insistence on the theoretical impossibility of voice, then this critical development matches a longer trajectory in the novel itself – away from a fiction which sought to maintain the idea that the narrator is able to speak to us, and towards a kind of writing which consistently exposed its own artificiality, its own emptiness of self and of voice.

III

There is much truth in this characterisation of the history of the novel, and the critical disavowal of voice that emerges in the 1960s is in some sense a response to this trajectory that had already been established in literary fiction. But what I want to explore here, in relation to our current understanding of the value of the novel, is the possibility that our recognition of this trajectory has made us inattentive to the ways in which voice persists from Defoe to George Eliot to

Beckett and beyond. The no doubt proper sense that the novel, over the course of its history, has become increasingly sceptical of the conditions of its own production has perhaps blinded us to two things: both to the fact that the realist novel, so called, was not uncritical of its own mimetic procedures, and to the fact that neither the modernist nor the postmodernist novel have completely freed themselves from the coils of such procedures. To focus on the present comparison between Dickens and Beckett, it might be that the novel voice in Dickens is not as committed to the reproduction of presence and self-identity as it has sometimes appeared to be; and it might be that Beckett's work, however much it empties or evacuates the narrative self, cannot quite free itself from the strains of the voice which, as George Eliot has put it, 'go deeper into us than other things'.[17] If there is some kind of remainder, some element of voice which theory has not dismantled, and which the novel itself has not silenced, then perhaps, in part, it is in the submerged vocal resonance I suggest we can detect between Beckett and Dickens that this remainder might lie.

One way to approach this resonance, this shared vocal ground, is to attend to the voice of the parent, as it is heard in both Dickens and Beckett, and to the related association in both writers between fathers and mothers and origins. This, of course, is to risk disturbing the shallow sleep of the most powerful ontotheological myth in the history of meta-physics, that which finds the origin of presence in the voice of the father. In the beginning, as John will tell you, was the Word, and the Word was God. But I risk this here not to posit any structural association between Christian theology and narrative voice, but to suggest that both Beckett and Dickens are fundamentally concerned with the way that voice gives rise to being in the imagined world of the novel. It is not the case, I think, that Dickens draws from voice, and from the voice of the father, some mythical or ontological grounds upon which to build his fictional world, or to stage some kind of recovered presence; nor is it the case that Beckett's writing simply reveals the absence of such grounds. Rather, I think that both writers offer extraordinarily powerful self-reflexive analyses of the ways in which their imagined worlds are shaped by a progenitive voice, analyses which, taken together, offer a kind of moving picture of the way that the novel voice works.

Now, whatever Dickens' investment in the paternal voice might be, it is notoriously the case that parents in Dickens are notable for their absence. The missing father is a recurrent obsession throughout *David Copperfield*, as he is in *Great Expectations*, *Bleak House* and elsewhere. This absence makes itself felt in many ways, but perhaps most intriguingly in what we might think of as a kind of nominative insufficiency. As David Copperfield recalls the scenes of his birth, six months after his father's death, into his family home, it is this insufficiency that insistently recurs. 'Looking back', he says, 'into the blank of my infancy', he is able to picture the house, even the scene of his birth: 'There comes out of the cloud', he says, 'our house – not new to me but quite familiar in its earliest remembrance' (p. 25). He cannot construct the house as a new or unfamiliar thing, even upon his first beholding it, so deeply is it woven into his remembrance of his childhood, so closely associated with the vaporous origin of self; but even as the house emerges in this way from the cloud of non-being as always already known, it carries in its signs for itself the trace of the father's absence. The house was named 'The Rookery' by the late David Copperfield, because, David's mother says, 'when he bought the house, he liked to think there were rooks about it' (p. 17). But, as David's indomitable aunt and surrogate parent remarks, there are in fact no rooks anywhere about the house. It is, the aunt tells us, in the only characterisation of Copperfield senior in the book, 'David Copperfield from head to foot!'. He 'calls a house a rookery when there's not a rook near it' (p. 18). As the house emerges in David's memory, this gap between name and thing, or this emptiness at the heart of named things, repeats itself; there is a 'back yard', he remembers, 'with a pigeon-house on a pole, in the centre, without any pigeons in it', and a 'great dog-kennel in a corner, without any dog' (p. 25). And throughout the novel, there is a recurrent disjuncture between signs and things, a heightened awareness of the possibility that the name does not quite capture the thing named, or sits at a peculiar, mistaken angle to it. Catching an echo of the misnamed rookery, David himself is misnamed, by the murderous Murdstone, as 'Brookes of Sheffield'; and the many other names that David is given through the narrative – Daisy, Davey, Doady, Trotwood, Mr Copperful – all suggest an ill fit between name and thing.

The way that we encounter presence in *David Copperfield* is shaped by this central schism or fault-line, this failure of the patrinominal glue that binds names and things. The rooks that failed to appear at the Blunderstone Rookery, that fled the scene of their naming, recur throughout the narrative, carrying with them always the ghost of the dead father, banished both from body and from name. In insistently recurring in this way, it might appear that the rooks – as emblems at once of the dead father and of his resistance to the proper name – are seeking some kind of return, some kind of re-entry to the novel's economy of signs. But what I think is intriguing about this fluttering, flighty non-appearance of the father, disguised under a false name – or, more accurately, named only by an original association with misnaming – is that it maintains its distance and its muteness; it achieves its paternal power not by speaking, but precisely by refusing to speak, or by marking the failure of the narrative voice to summon it to presence. The father does not seek embodiment, but instead shelters in a kind of shaped absence in the text, a recess of a kind which the narrator defends against the threat or irruption of presence. The arrival of Mr Murdstone, the hated stepfather, offers just such a threat, presenting to David the ghastly spectacle of the father made flesh. Murdstone's presence, his physical manifestation, is evoked with palpable disgust. His black hair and brows, strong beard and fleshy white face make him appear as a kind of superabundance of pale, doughy stuff. Murdstone's presence overwhelms David's mother, and it threatens also to saturate the narrative itself, to swamp those delicate recesses where the father lives on, unknown and unnamed. When David first discovers that Murdstone has moved in to his home, he finds at the same time that one of those treasured repositories of namelessness has been brutally stuffed (in an ugly echo of the nuptials). He finds, as he wanders disconsolately in the yard, that the 'empty dog-kennel was filled up with a great dog – deep mouthed and black-haired like Him' (p. 55).

The arrival of Murdstone – the first of many scenes of parental substitution in *David Copperfield* – is doubtless the most brutal. As the novel continues David learns to adapt to fatherlessness, and to train himself to accept the skewed relationship between names and things that is his father's legacy to him. But what I want most centrally to argue here is that, as David makes his journey towards himself, he maintains that absence that inhabits the name in this novel. He defends it as the site of a kind of latent aesthetic potential – the very possibility of narrative – rather than as an insufficiency that must be overcome. The voices that come to supplement that absence at the origin – the voice of the mother, of Agnes, the narrator's own voice – all turn around a cherished, guarded silence, a muteness which is threaded into the strains of the voice itself, and which makes an intrinsic part of the voice that we hear when we read. David finds his love both of Agnes and of his mother preserved in the particular pitch and modulation of their voices. 'There was always something in her modest voice', David says of Agnes, 'that seemed to touch a chord within me, answering to that sound alone' (p. 374). But even as he responds inwardly to the music of voice, this musicality contains within it something that cannot be sounded, a kind of unspeakable remainder which troubles the very conception of an inner being that is fully present to itself. When David returns to his childhood home to find that his mother and Murdstone have had a child, this remainder, this absence in the homeland of the voice, is given its most poignant expression. David hears his mother singing as he enters the house, not yet knowing that she had become a mother again, not yet knowing that she was singing not to him, but to someone who has taken his place. 'God knows', he says as he hears her voice,

> how infantine the memory may have been, that was awakened within me by the sound of my mother's voice in the old parlor, when I set foot in the hall. She was singing in a low tone. I think I must have lain in her arms, and heard her singing so to me when I was a baby. The strain was new to me, and yet it was so old that it filled my heart brim-full; like a friend come back from a long absence. (p. 121)

The voice of the mother calls here to that earliest self, the self who can only register newness – the newness of the house, the newness of the parent's voice – as something infinitely ancient, always already known. This is a fantasised self that has known no absence, no lack. But in singing this ancient song, the mother demonstrates to David that this call is never addressed to us alone, and never quite strikes that chord within us, that inner place where we have our most secret being. David longs at this moment to become his baby brother, to find himself secreted within himself by becoming the addressee of that voice. He lies 'upon her bosom near the little creature', so that 'her eyes looking down upon its face' should also look down upon him; and he experiences briefly the feeling of presence that such a gaze seems to bestow, that feeling of having one's heart 'brim-full'. 'I wish I had died', he says, 'I wish I had died then, with that feeling in my heart' (p. 121). But the burden of his narrative, the experience of guiding himself towards his own mature self, carried only by his own voice, is the recognition that this fullness is not available to him. This is not how we make ourselves from the resources of our own narration. His mother's cryptic parting gesture to him as he drives away from her for the last time – he last sees her standing 'at the garden gate alone, holding her baby up in her arms for me to see' (p. 133) – tells him as much. In heading towards himself, he leaves this infantine version of himself behind, the version summoned into being by the sound of the mother's loving voice. When mother and baby die, David tells himself he has had his wish, that he too has died, with that brim-fullness in his heart. 'The mother who lay in the grave', he thinks, 'was the mother of my infancy; the little creature in her arms, was myself, as I had once been, hushed for ever on her bosom' (p. 144). But if this is death, then it is death into narrative, death into the experience of partial being that is the only kind of birth that the narrative voice, composite of sound and silence, can give to itself.

Insofar as narrative voice in *David Copperfield*, and in Dickens' novels more generally, seeks to conjure a kind of presence, then it is this partial presence, this coming to being that is inhabited by an emptiness, an originary lack, that it evokes. The very condition of narrative voice, its phenomenological and aesthetic architecture, means that it carries a forsaking within it. When David reflects on what he calls the 'making' of 'his imaginative world' (p. 180), he recognises that the voice cannot constitute this world as a whole, cannot make it into a haven in which he will find a home. Rather, he dwells throughout on the tendency of body, place and voice to disassemble themselves, to re-stage that self-estrangement, that recognition of self as other, that happens so poignantly as David listens to his mother singing. Those moments when the body comes most strikingly asunder – when young David falls asleep as his school master plays his hypnotic flute, for example, or when he experiences his first bout of drunkenness – are not exceptions to the rule of bodily inhabitation in Dickens but the norm, the very condition of narrative being. As young David begins to nod off to the strains of the flute, his 'imaginative world' fades, to leave a yawning blank that is the evacuated ground of being in the novel, the always empty space intervening between narrator and narrated. 'She fades', he says, 'he fades, and all fades, and there is no flute, no master, no Salem House, no David Copperfield' (p. 88). And as he gets drunker during what he calls his 'first dissipation', he traces with exquisite comic touch the snapping of the bonds that hold the narrative world together, that bind young David to himself. 'Somebody was leaning out of my bed-room window, refreshing his forehead against the cool stone of the parapet', he says. 'It was myself.' 'Now', he goes on, 'somebody was unsteadily contemplating his features in the looking-glass. That was I too.' And of his subsequent passage down the stairs, he says 'near the bottom, somebody fell, and rolled down. Somebody else said it was Copperfield. I was angry at that false report, until, finding myself on my back in the passage, I began to think that there might be some foundation for it' (p. 370). This body in parts, this being at a remove from itself, this is the condition of narrative invention in Dickens. It is this continually moving difference between self and self, the continual failure of the narrator to take full ownership of himself, that is the still breath on which the narrative voice is carried. Such insufficiency is not an epistemological void that the voice must banish by its claims to presence or omniscience, but the delicate blindness woven into sight, silence woven into sound, non-being woven into being, that is the very condition of the novel voice.

It is perhaps in its re-appearance in the work of Samuel Beckett, a century and more later, that we might see the strange persistence of this balance between sound and silence as it is woven into the phenomenology of narrative voice. The scenario that Dickens presents, in which a speaking I only partly shares its being with the I of which it speaks – in which the speaking I seeks to become its own parent, to give partial and fitful birth to itself as character – this is the archetypal scenario in Beckett's fiction. It is not, perhaps, that Beckett strips the novel of its characteristic features – that he takes the fully realised imaginative world he inherits from Dickens and others, and dismantles it, steering it from voice to silence, from light to dark. Rather, what Beckett offers is a distillation of a novelistic condition, a starker, more naked depiction of a kind of ur-predicament that one finds also in Dickens, in Eliot. It is perhaps the case, as Maurice Blanchot has suggested, that 'works such as these, and first of all Beckett's, come closer than is customary to the movement of writing and the movement of reading', that with a work such as *How It Is*, 'we have returned to the source of the novel'.[18] Where, in Dickens' novels, the peculiar junction between voice and silence is hidden deep within the folds of the text so that we have to gently part them to see it, in Beckett's work it is precisely this that is revealed, thrust into view. As Malone oversees the death of his storytelling, as an effect of his own dying, it is this strange suture, this exploded bridge between narrator and character, that he strives to show us. 'I began again', he says, to undergo the trials of narration, 'to be another, in myself, in another'. But 'little by little' he goes on, as his decrepitude overcomes him, he undertakes this journey towards himself as other 'with a different aim, no longer in order to succeed but in order to fail'.[19] He seeks not to maintain the illusion of presence, the illusion of identity between narrator and character, not to find himself, as an earlier Beckett narrator puts it, 'bedded in my old flesh'.[20] Rather, he seeks to expose the mechanics of the process by which the striving for identity in narrative endlessly fails, releasing him to a kind of suspended emptiness, allowing him, as he puts it, to 'die alive'. 'What I sought', he says,

> when I struggled out of my hole, then aloft through the stinging air towards an inaccessible boon, was the rapture of vertigo, the letting go, the fall, the gulf, the relapse to darkness, to nothingness. (p. 195)

What Malone seeks is not to be at one with himself, not to find himself, like David, returned to an infantine fullness of self, lying on his mother's breast, beneath her loving gaze; rather, he sets out to relive the ejection from such selfhood into the freedom of narrative absence, the freedom into which David is cast as he heads away from that graven image of his mother holding his small self aloft. He wills that ejection from the mother's dwelling place that glimmers in the opening line of *Molloy*. But what is so striking about this will in *Malone Dies* is that it opens onto a strange persistence of the very elements that it seeks to eradicate. With the relapse to nothingness comes not simply silence, but an inrush of paternal presence, a reassertion of that very paternal geist that is not cancelled by the urge towards nothingness, but finds its unspeakable home there. As the above passage runs on, it moves seamlessly from self-abnegation to a kind of prayer to a loving, missing father. He seeks, Malone says,

> the relapse to darkness, to nothingness, to earnestness, to home, to him waiting for me always, who needed me and whom I needed, who took me in his arms and told me to stay with him always, who gave me his place and watched over me, who suffered every time I left him, whom I have often made suffer and seldom contented, whom I have never seen. (p. 195)

Again and again, as Beckett's narrative structures tighten and sparsen after the word frenzy of *Malone Dies* and *The Unnamable*, we see this effect re-emerging as the underlying condition of narrative voice. The more forcefully the speaking narrator seeks to free himself from the architecture of his own utterance, the more forcefully this architecture reasserts itself. In *Texts for Nothing*, in *How It Is*, in the agonisingly short prose of the sixties and seventies, Beckett's narrator sets up narrative systems in order to allow them to fail, to allow them to commit a kind of suicide, which releases him from the requirement that he should speak, that he should go through the terror of self-loss that is the experience of self-enunciation. And in each case, the collapse of the narrative system leads not to some final release from voice, but to a fresh encounter with it, as the origin and remainder of the narrative scenario, an original remainder that cannot be eradicated – a remainder that is, as a late narrator puts it, 'unlessenable'.[21]

In an oddly sentimental scenario that recurs in *The Calmative* and *Texts for Nothing*, Beckett's narrator imagines this struggle to free himself from voice as a version of the process by which his father would lull him to sleep, when he was a child, by reading to him every night the same story – the story of Joe Breem or Breen, the son of a lighthouse keeper. 'This evening', the narrator of *The Calmative* says, 'it has to be as in the story my father used to read me, evening after evening, when I was small, and he had all his health, to calm me' (p. 53). The story that the narrator tells himself, he says, will calm him in the same way, will send him to a sleep in which he can free himself from himself, free himself from the narrating scenario into the calm sleep of childhood, that sleep that Dickens' David succumbs to as he listens to his teacher's flute, a sleep in which 'he fades, she fades, and all fades'. As the narrator of *Texts for Nothing* puts it, he tells himself stories, 'to lull me and keep me company', as 'when my father took me on his knee and read me the one about Joe Breem, or Breen';[22] and in these stories, the narrator plays the part both of father and of son, both he who talks and he who listens. 'I'm in my arms', he says, 'I'm holding myself in my arms, without much tenderness, but faithfully, faithfully' (p. 104). And in this embrace – as David lies in the dead embrace of his mother, as he is inhabited by the voice of himself as his own father – Beckett's narrator imagines that he might 'Sleep now, as under that ancient lamp, all twined together, tired out with so much talking, so much listening' (p. 104). But, as David's deathly sleep only projects him into the narrative condition of partial being, of a voice which speaks in a language composed of silence rather than quenched by it, so the narrator of *Texts for Nothing* recognises that to sleep is to return to the lap of an endless and ancient voice, a voice that is familiar at first hearing, but that he has never heard. At those moments of calm and sleep, the narrator says, one might think that 'there is only silence'; but this is true only to the extent that it is untrue, as this silence is that which inhabits the narrative voice; a silence which sounds even as the voice is in full flow, just as the voice infests the silence even after it has ceased to speak. 'It's true', the narrator says, 'it's true and it's not true, there is silence and there is not silence, there is no one and there is someone . . . . And were the voice to cease quite at last, the old ceasing voice, it would not be true, as it is not true that it speaks, it can't speak, it can't cease' (p. 154).

It is this voice, that can't speak and can't cease, composed at once of sound and silence, that I suggest we might call the novel voice, the voice that we can hear when we read. It is this voice, as Mladen Dolar has recently argued, that is the 'element that ties the subject and the Other together, without belonging to either'.[23] It is this voice that goes on, even after the novel has rid itself of its illusionistic devices, even after half a century of theoretical work has helped to rid us of the pervasive myth that writing recreates speech as the province of spiritual self-presence. If, as Andrew Gibson argues, we have found it difficult, in our 'post-theoretical' age, to find a way '*not* to hear' narrative voice, if narrative continues to be bound up with voice, even in the full understanding that it is the 'tomb of speech' rather than its preservative, it is perhaps because the novel touches, in the most intimate way, on this ineradicable boundary between sound and silence, being and non-being. The novel does not contain voice – as Fludernik says, it is 'not a tape recording'. But it does bring us closer than any other medium or art form to the process by which we make ourselves out of the stories we tell ourselves, the process by which we 'make' our 'imaginative world'. In hearing the novel, we are of course hearing our own voice, hearing the process by which consciousness binds itself, with the utmost fragility, to material being, the process by which we tell ourselves who and what we are and were. For the novel voice to approach this most intimate, most hidden of infinite conversations, it does not need to pretend that it can speak. The novels that achieve the most searing proximity to our self-making mechanisms are those that hear their own silence, and live in the rather terrible gap, endlessly opening and as endlessly closing, between words and things, speaking and listening. The speaker and the hearer, in Beckett and in Dickens, the spoken word and the silent, they are 'all twined together'; it is this twining that allows us to suffer the privilege of living. But they also and forever come asunder, which allows us to hear the tombal silence of spoken words, and endlessly to perform the binding that is reading, thinking, being.

2   Is This Really Realism?

I wonder whether one oftener learns to love real objects through their representations, or the representations through the real objects.

George Eliot, *Daniel Deronda*[1]

The image is not the duplicate of a thing. It is a complex set of relations between the visible and the invisible, the visible and speech, the said and the unsaid.

Jacques Rancière, *The Emancipated Spectator*[2]

I

In the last chapter I suggested that our understanding of narrative voice – that fundamental formal property of the novel – is now entering a transformative phase. To understand how the novel works today – to understand what we mean by the value of the novel – we need to develop a new way of thinking about the novel voice, a new way of hearing it. If this is true, then it is so to the extent that the broader formal apparatus of the novel, of which the voice might be thought of as only one element, is also entering a crisis, in which its most essential attributes have to be rethought. I mean, of course, the formal category of realism, the mode which is so closely associated with the novel that the two – realism and the novel – have sometimes appeared mutually to define one another. It is the novel that allows us fully to conceive of realism, and it is the urge towards realism that has shaped the passage of the novel, from its earliest beginnings. As Georg Lukács has put it, 'realism is not one style among others', but, rather, 'all writing must contain a certain degree of realism'. 'All styles', he writes, '(even those seemingly most opposed to realism) originate in it or are significantly related to it'.[3] There is a 'tendency', Fredric Jameson has recently argued, both 'to identify realism with the novel itself' and to think of the 'history of the novel' as 'inevitably the history of the realist novel, against which or underneath which all the aberrant modes, such as the fantastic novel or the episodic novel, are subsumed'.[4]

The history of the novel is entwined with the history of realism, to the extent that they define one another; and yet, as I say, the question of what we mean by realism – what its value or purpose is, and how the novel is seen to practice it – has fallen today into a kind of suspension or quite radical uncertainty. It may be the case that realism has always been peculiarly resistant to the critical gaze. Jameson notes this resistance at the opening of his 2013 work *The Antinomies of Realism*, observing that whenever 'we attempt to hold the phenomenon of realism firmly in our mind's eye', it is 'as though the object of our meditation began to wobble' (p. 1). Realism itself is reluctant to come into view, perhaps because, as the structuring principle which allows us to see or picture the world, it must keep itself hidden – the Higgs boson particle of the represented universe. But if this elusive quality is native to realism itself, it is also the case, I think, that we are now at a juncture in the history of our response to realism, at which our capacity to critically comprehend or apprehend it is particularly attenuated.

Critical comments on realism by two contemporary novelists, both of whom are implicitly reflecting on their own practice as novelists, will serve to characterise the problem I have in mind. The first comes from the South African novelist J.M. Coetzee, and his 2003 novel *Elizabeth Costello*. This work consists of a series of 'lessons' built around lectures given by the eponymous character, Elizabeth Costello, a novelist who stands in some fashion as a fictional mouthpiece for Coetzee himself. The first of these 'lessons' suggests the kind of difficulty with our understanding of realism that I have in mind here. It depicts a scenario in which Costello gives a public lecture entitled 'What is Realism', in which she discusses Franz Kafka's story

'Report to an Academy'. She is interested in this story, she says, because it marks a decisive moment in the history of realism, a moment at which one of the shared assumptions that make realism possible suddenly expires or reveals itself to have been based all along on a false premise. 'Report to an Academy' tells the story of an ape – named 'Red Peter' – who gives a public lecture to a learned society, in which he describes the painful process by which he acquired language, became educated, and learnt to adopt the dress, mannerisms and beliefs of a human being. What is striking about this story in relation to the question 'what is realism?', Costello argues in her own address to a learned society, is that its formal properties allow us no purchase on its truth value, no capacity to gauge the nature of its realism. 'If you know the story', Costello says, 'you will remember that it is cast in the form of a monologue, a monologue by the ape', and, as a result, we can achieve no objective perspective on the story that the ape tells. 'Within this form', Costello says,

> there is no means for either speaker or audience to be inspected with an outsider's eye. For all we know, the speaker may not "really" be an ape, may be simply a human being like ourselves deluded into thinking himself an ape, or a human being presenting himself, with heavy irony for rhetorical purposes, as an ape.[5]

The metafictional charge to this moment in Coetzee's novel is explicit. At the opening of her lecture, Costello draws attention to the parallels between her own situation and Red Peter's: 'Why am I reminding you of Kafka's story?', she asks. 'Am I going to pretend I am the ape, torn away from my natural surroundings, forced to perform in front of a gathering of critical strangers?' (p. 18). As Kafka's story leaves us in the dark – as we don't know 'what is going on in this story: whether it is about a man speaking to men or an ape speaking to apes or an ape speaking to men or a man speaking to apes, or even just a parrot speaking to parrots' (p. 19) – so Costello's lecture takes place in a suspended relation to reality. Is Elizabeth Costello 'really' J.M. Coetzee? Is what we are reading really a lecture on realism, rather than a novel? Or is it more properly a lecture on animal rights, which is only pretending to be a lecture on realism? Or is it a lecture pretending to be a novel pretending to be a lecture, which pretends to be on realism while it is really on animal rights? These questions remain unanswered in *Elizabeth Costello*, just as they remain unanswered in 'Report to an Academy', because, Costello argues, Kafka's work marks the point at which these kinds of discrimination, between fiction and reality, between realism and its opposite, become difficult to sustain. 'There used to be a time', Costello argues, when we could make these distinctions, when we could test the difference between a true and a false statement about the world, and when our conception of ourselves and others could rest securely on this established difference. 'We used to believe that when the text said, "on the table stood a glass of water," there was indeed a table, and a glass of water on it, and we had only to look in the word-mirror of the text to see them'. But those days, she says, have gone: 'All that has ended. The word-mirror is broken, irreparably, it seems .... The words on the page will no longer stand up and be counted, each proclaiming "I mean what I mean"' (p. 19). It appears that the language tools that allow us to describe ourselves and others, to differentiate between a man and a woman, between a human and an ape, between a true report and a false one, are not only broken beyond repair, but they have always been broken, have never really been able to accomplish the tasks that we thought they were doing so well, for so many centuries. 'There used to be a time, we believe, when we could say who we were', Costello says, but now 'we are just performers speaking our parts' (p. 19). And as we recognise the untruth of all our speech acts, all our beliefs about ourselves and the world, we realise that we cannot even mourn the certainty that we have lost, because this has turned out never to have been certain at all. 'The bottom has dropped out', Costello says. 'We could think of this as a tragic turn of events, were it not that it is hard to have respect for whatever was the bottom that dropped out – it looks to us like an illusion now, one of those illusions shared by everyone in the room' (pp. 19–20).

For J.M. Coetzee, then, or for J.M. Coetzee speaking as Elizabeth Costello, something drastic happens to our capacity to apprehend and represent the real at some point in the twentieth century. This something drastic either originates in or is captured by Kafka's fiction, in which the imagination is dissociated from the world, cast into a darkness in which it is impossible to find one's bearings, or to orient oneself to the guiding co-ordinates of human being. After Kafka's work, Costello implies, literary fiction has to reckon with the fact that realism is no longer possible, that the very basis of realistic representation – the very idea that words are able to represent objects in the world – has suffered a catastrophic failure.

The lecture hall in *Elizabeth Costello* – the imagined academic arena in which this reflection on the end of realism takes place – suffers from precisely the kind of suspension that Costello finds in 'Report to an Academy': the suspension of the forces which allow us to differentiate between human and animal, between the true and the false. In *Elizabeth Costello*, as in 'Report to an Academy', Costello says, 'The lecture hall itself may be nothing but a zoo' (p. 19). If fiction after Kafka is possible at all, if it is able to reflect on the conditions of its own possibility, then it can only do so in this strangely self-obliterating way, can only speak in a voice that sounds its own silence, or that reveals its own groundlessness, its own loss of species.

The second comment which I want to address here might seem to imply more or less the opposite view of the fate of contemporary realism. Zadie Smith, in her 2008 essay 'Two Directions for the Novel', suggests that, rather than suffering some kind of fundamental collapse somewhere in the twentieth century, realism is in fact the most extraordinarily resilient of literary modes, and the challenge to its dominance that was represented by Kafka and other twentieth-century high modernists made scarcely a dent in its bumper. Smith's essay proceeds by a comparison between two contemporary novels – Joseph O'Neill's *Netherland* and Tom McCarthy's *Remainder*. The first of these, she suggests, is a contemporary example of 'lyrical realism', based on what she calls the 'Balzac–Flaubert model',[6] in which the world is captured, in all its colour and fullness, by the turns of O'Neill's stylish, prettified prose. The second is a difficult experimental novel that refuses the consolations of lyricism and deliberately undermines our sense that the world would allow itself to be tamely captured by a well-crafted sentence. Smith offers this comparison in order to argue that the kinds of challenge to a complacent realism that emerged in modernism and postmodernism have now, under contemporary market conditions, faded away, yielding the ground once more to a tired and faded Balzac–Flaubert formula. McCarthy's difficult, trenchant novel took seven years to find a publisher, Smith tells us, because it had to buck the trend of a marketplace that cannot allow anything other than O'Neill's lyrical realism to flourish. 'The Literary economy', she writes, 'sets up its stall on the road that leads to *Netherland*'. This road is the one 'along which one might wave to Jane Austen, George Eliot, F. Scott Fitzgerald, Richard Yates'. This is the tradition of safe realism to which O'Neill belongs, and which currently corners the market. Rarely, she argues, has the publishing industry been less interested 'in seeing what's new on the route to *Remainder*, that skewed side road where we meet Georges Perec, Clarice Lispector, Maurice Blanchot, William Burroughs, J.G. Ballard' (p. 93). These latter writers, along with others who sit at an angle to the 'Balzac–Flaubert model' – Smith names Melville, Conrad, Kafka, Beckett, Joyce and Nabokov – have offered some kind of challenge to the tenets of literary realism, in terms that echo Costello's remarks on Kafka's fiction. There is a tradition of literary and theoretical critiques of nineteenth-century lyrical realism, which are grounded in a 'scepticism of realism's metaphysical tendencies', and which 'peaked in that radical deconstructive doubt that questions the capacity of language itself to describe the world in any accuracy' (p. 73). Yet, despite this tradition, which saw its final flourishes in the American postmodernism of Barth, Pynchon, Gaddis and David Foster Wallace, we have now resumed business as usual. The 'opposition to realism' represented by the critical tradition that runs from Melville to Wallace has been safely defused, Smith writes, and the 'last man standing is the Balzac–Flaubert model, on the evidence of its extraordinary persistence' (p. 73).

So, both Coetzee and Smith offer versions of the same crisis. Fiction has lost the capacity to accurately represent the world, and it has also outlived the excitement that the recognition of this loss occasioned, the excitement that drove first the modernism of Woolf, Joyce and Kafka, and then the postmodernism of Barth, Pynchon and Wallace. We are left either with the picture presented by Coetzee – in which the Kafkan novelist lives on after the end of modernism, becoming ever more remote from a world with which it has no cultural or representational tie – or that presented by Smith – in which the realist novelist resumes the business of telling stories about the world, in the half knowledge that such storytelling is inauthentic and politically and aesthetically bankrupt. And, for both writers, the implicit challenge is to find a way past this impasse, a way to reconceive the task of the novelist, so that he or she can engage critically and poetically with the world once more, without resorting to the tinselly consolations of a lyrical realism that belongs to an earlier historical moment. One can see now, throughout the literary critical sphere, the stirrings of a desire to re-apprehend the real, a desire to find new forms with which to examine reality, now that the postmodern moment seems, in some sense, to have come to an end. There is in our time, as Peter Brooks has recently put it, 'a thirst for reality' – or, in David Shields' terms, a 'reality hunger'.[7] As Hal Foster has recently argued, one can see what has been called the 'return of the real' across the critical arts.[8] But the challenge for us now is to find a way of responding to this desire, to this hunger, this thirst, without simply re-animating dead categories, without unlearning the lessons that we have been taught by modernism and by deconstruction, without unthinking the thoughts that made the twentieth century a revolutionary time for the literary mind. Zadie Smith, despite her fulminations against lyrical realism, admits that she has 'written in this tradition myself', and that she 'cautiously hope[s] for its survival' (p. 80). It is not so much the end of realism that Smith wants, as a means of making realism work once more, in the light of the difficult knowledge about the world that we have inherited from Woolf, from Kafka, from Lispector, from Derrida. If lyrical realism is to survive, Smith writes, 'lyrical realists will have to push a little harder on their subject' (p. 80), will have to transform the modes in which they imagine the world, rather than half-heartedly patching up those which they find in the attic, left behind by the previous owners. Whatever happened in the last century to give the impression that the 'word-mirror had been broken' was not a blip, not a time-out, not a lapse from sanity and common sense; it was a deeply transformative moment in the passage of intellectual, political and aesthetic history, and one which demands a response from those who come in its wake. If one of the legacies of this transformation, for us now, is the collective hunger and thirst for the real, then it falls to the novelists and theorists of our time to find a way of articulating this need, in forms made available by our time, and not in those cut and fashioned by an earlier generation. If we need now to rethink the meaning of contemporary realism, we cannot simply reheat Lukács' critical vocabulary – a terminology and methodology fashioned as a defence against the emerging threat of modernism – any more than we can reproduce the prose of Flaubert or Balzac. We need now a realism, both in practice and in theory, that emerges from the aesthetic discoveries of the last century rather than defending itself against them, and that engages dialectically with the economic, cultural and material forces that produce reality today.

II

To begin to respond to these demands – to address the question of the value of the novel today by rethinking its capacity to offer a critical representation of reality – requires us, I think, to ask again what we mean by the term realism, to try once more to hold the 'phenomenon' in 'our mind's eye', despite its tendency, as observed by Jameson, for it to 'wobble'. Zadie Smith asks, of the realism that she finds rehearsed in O'Neill's purple prose, 'Is this really realism?', and it is worth, I think, dwelling for a while on this question, and on what Smith means by it. 'Is this really what having a self feels like?', she asks; 'is this how memory works? ... Is this how time feels?' (p. 81), and in presenting these rhetorical questions, she implies that the kind of literature she opposes to lyrical realism in her essay – the kind that runs from Melville through B.S. Johnson to Tom McCarthy – is actually better at representing reality than realism is. The self is not 'essentially full and continuous' (p. 73), as the conventions of realism dictate that it should be. Rather, the self is a 'tenuous' thing (p. 80), and it *feels* to us tenuous, just as the world does not come to us in a well composed and balanced picture, in harmony with our moods and desires, but rather in a series of discordant, difficult, violent experiences that cannot be properly assembled together. Life is more like a jump cut than a continuity edit, more like the *nouvelle vague* than Hollywood. So, an art work that is discontinuous and violent, one that empties out the experience of selfhood rather than seeking to shore it up, this is actually a more 'real' kind of art. Surely, Smith suggests, if we are interested in what it really feels like to have a self then we should turn not to Balzac, or to Flaubert, or to George Eliot, but to Kafka, to Beckett, to Ballard.

In suggesting this kind of opposition Smith is rehearsing a well-established convention, one that is present too in Costello's sketch of literary history. The realism with which we might identify the rise of the eighteenth-century novel (Defoe, Swift, Wollstonecraft, Fielding), which emerges in its present guise in the French novel of the nine-teenth century (Balzac, Flaubert, Zola), and which dominates the English novel, the American novel, the European novel, throughout the eighteenth and nineteenth centuries, and into the twentieth – this is an essentially naive form, which proceeds on the basis of a kind of category error and relies on a set of assumptions which have turned out to be mistaken. The great realists composed their works on the understanding that language and reality had some kind of common basis, that looking at representations of the world (in painting, in literature) help us to understand the world represented, as representa-tion is bound to the world by some kind of metaphysical glue. But, a moment comes, Smith writes, when we realise that 'the world has changed and we do not stand in the same relation to it as we did when Balzac was writing' (p. 76). Balzac's novel *Père Goriot* is built around the naive assumption that the outside world is a mirror of the internal world of the character's minds. But the move from nineteenth-century realism to the modernism of the twentieth century – along with the associated advent of twentieth-century critical theory, from Saussure to Barthes to Derrida – cures us of this naivety. When the mirror shatters, when the bottom drops out, then the scales fall from our eyes and we realise that the realism that the novel has given us isn't really realism after all, and that it takes a different kind of art – an art alive to the gap between word and thing, and to the arbitrary relation between signifier and signified – to capture real reality, a reality in which 'the words on the page will no longer stand up and be counted, each proclaiming "I mean what I mean"'.

This account of literary history, or a version of it, is implied in Smith's rhetorical question 'Is this really realism?' But what I want to suggest here, in focusing on this question, is two things: firstly, that this sketch of the relationship between realism and anti-realism is based on a partial and reductive understanding of 'lyrical realism', of the 'Balzac-Flaubert model'; and, secondly, that this kind of inaccuracy, this tendency to parody or caricature 'realism' in order to champion its opposite, is not simply an error or a misreading, but an urge that is native to realism itself, and one which contains within it the seeds of realism's future, of the novel's future. If we are to see our way past the impasse in which we find ourselves now – in which a reawakened hunger for the real is combined with a crisis in the authenticity of the realist modes in which we might represent it – we have to respond to Smith's question in two ways. We have not simply to produce a more accurate, less caricatured model for understanding how the history of prose realism has sought to make pictures of the world. We have also to develop an understanding of how a dissatisfaction with realism, a sense that realism is never really realism, is the result not of an aberration, not of a failure of the mechanisms of realism, but part of its basic condition, and its means of going on.

I will begin with the first of these two tasks – the reappraisal of what we mean by realism, of what realism "really" is – by looking back, from Kafka to Defoe. Kafka's work, both Smith and Coetzee's Costello suggest, is a manifestation of some recognition that the basis upon which literary realism rests is in some sense faulty. This is, as I have said, a common enough argument, and tends to cast the modern and contemporary imagination as enlightened, in contrast to the benighted ones who came before us, who had no idea, in their simplicity, that reality is constructed rather than given. But, whilst this narrative might be effective as a way of thinking about modern and contemporary fiction, it is based on a misrepresentation of the ways in which reality is represented in literary fiction throughout its history, a misrepresentation which reveals itself plainly the moment that one reads any novel that precedes Kafka or Joyce or Woolf. There is no moment, I would argue, in the history of the novel, at which the question of representation, the question of the relationship between reality and our pictures of it, has not been a fraught one; and what is more, there is no moment at which this fraught relationship has not been the central business of the novel to address.

Indeed, one might suggest that one of the founding texts of the modern realist novel – Daniel Defoe's *Robinson Crusoe* (1719) – is nothing more than an exercise in anxiety, a panicky and shaky attempt to find a means of producing a stable account of the world that is every bit as uncertain about the capacity of words to 'stand up and be counted' as anything by Kafka. Defoe's novel has been read, famously, as marking the moment when the emergence of capitalist modernity coincided with the appearance of the modern novel as a form, giving rise to the discursive, ideological apparatus which has shaped contemporary reality. The novel tells the story of Crusoe's shipwreck and his long exile on a desert island, during which time he creates a micro-version of a modern sovereign state, building himself a number of dwelling places, laboriously fashioning tools and boats out of hard wood, becoming a small-scale farmer, and finally making subjects out of stray visitors to his island (including most famously 'man Friday'), before eventually escaping from the island twenty-eight years after his arrival. In telling this story, according to Ian Watt's classic account of *Crusoe*, Defoe marks at once the shift from a feudalist to a capitalist world view, and the arrival of the novel as a mode of storytelling which is adapted to the conditions of this emergent cultural moment. Crusoe's shipwreck is a *literal* result of the expansion of colonial networks in the early period of European imperialism; it is during his pursuit of colonial trade that Crusoe suffers the shipwreck which casts him away on his island. But the novel is also, for Watt, a *metaphorical* response to this moment in European colonialism. In casting Crusoe away, Watt argues, Defoe examines the emergence of a kind of essential solitude that comes as a by-product of capitalism, and that evolves in the early eighteenth century into the condition of modern economic and social individualism. Modernity begins when the individual is removed from the theological and feudal networks of early modernity and forced to make a world out of his or her own resources. The modern novel arrives at this point too, as the form best suited to this task. 'It is appropriate', Watt writes, 'that the tradition of the novel should begin with a work [*Robinson Crusoe*] that annihilated the relationships of the traditional social order', because it is with this annihilation, this wiping clean of the slate, that the novel can begin its work of creating a new *weltanschauung*. The 'terms of the novel', he goes on, 'and of modern thought alike were established when the old order of moral and social relationships was shipwrecked, with Robinson Crusoe, by the rising tide of individualism'.[9] The novel arises, for Watt, at the moment that an older moral and social order is cleared away by the emergence of capitalist modernity – and the form that the novel employs to build a new 'network of personal relationships' is realism (p. 92). Where Defoe's predecessor Bunyan cast his stories of trials and tribulations in terms of allegory, in which the striving of the pilgrim is subsumed always into a larger, transcendent framework, Defoe crafts a radically new realist form in which shovels remain shovels and refuse bluntly to be trans-substantiated, or conjured into a symbol of suffering or toil. Defoe employs an unadorned, realist form in *Robinson Crusoe*, Watt argues, in order to depict the process by which humankind, under early eighteenth-century conditions, makes for itself a new rational order, out of the blunt raw materials to hand. As J. Donald Crowley puts it, glossing Watt, where Bunyan's 'richly colloquial realism' is 'always subject to the allegorical imperative', Defoe develops a realism that is 'so explicit, its focus so much on the irreducible physicality of objects and events, that it seems incapable of referring to an emblematic significance behind those objects and events'.[10]

Watt's is still one of the most influential accounts of *Crusoe* as an early example of prose realism, and it remains a powerful reading of the novel. But what I want to argue here is that the realism that Defoe develops in *Crusoe* – however explicit, however committed to the materiality of its objects – is not founded on anything like confidence in the relationship between language and the world; that on the contrary, the process by which Crusoe seeks to tame the world in which he finds himself is beset with the most sickly anxiety, and is constantly brought up against the stubborn refusal of things to yield to the names that we seek to give them. If Crusoe, as Watt argues, is charged by Defoe with the task of constructing a new means of seeing the world, of developing the formal mode in which capitalist modernity might make an image of itself, then the basis for this seeing is a deeply troubled one that completely fails to establish that snug fit between sign and thing that Smith finds in Balzac. This is nowhere more evident than in Crusoe's description of his own narrative procedures – his own account of the way that he comes to represent his condition to himself in language. Crusoe realises early on that in order to live on the island, in order to make that hostile environment into a dwelling place, he needs to shape it with language, and specifically with written language. The story of his stay on the island is really a story of transformation as an act of sovereign will – an account of the arduous labour that it takes to make a tree into a chair with his bare hands, and of the various other ingenious ways in which Crusoe bends the world to his will to convert a barren, wasted existence into an ordered, rational one. And at the heart of this act of will is the process of notation and description, an activity that is as arduous and painstaking, in its way, as the making of a shovel out of iron wood. Crusoe realises, after he has been on the island 'about Ten or Twelve days', that narration is his only hope of maintaining some kind of orientation in time and space, that the colonisation of his island requires him to convert the vast indifferentiation of time and space that lies before him – the blank temporal and spatial horizon – into some kind of story. His chief fear, after the terror of being eaten by ravenous beasts or cannibals, is 'that I should lose my Reckoning of Time for want of Books and Pen and Ink, and should even forget the Sabbath Days from the Working Days'.[11] So at first he establishes the most rudimentary form of notation, by carving an account of his predicament upon a 'great Cross' that he fashions out of wood, which records that '*I came on shore here on the 30th of* Sept. 1659'; and on this cross he makes a form of calendar, by 'cutting every Day a Notch with my Knife', to keep a 'weekly, monthly, and yearly reckoning of time' (p. 64). This early form of inscription, roughly chiselled into a crucifix, allows Crusoe to maintain a loose kind of contact with Christian time, to keep in touch with that version of history which takes us from Genesis to Revelations. But as he gathers goods from the ship and sets up a little store of ink, he manages to develop more elaborate written accounts of his condition, and so begins to exert a kind of intellectual mastery over his surroundings, and over himself. As soon as he has the ink to do so, he says,

> I drew up the State of my Affairs in Writing, not so much to leave them to any that were to come after me, for I was like to have but few Heirs, as to deliver my Thoughts from daily poring upon them, and afflicting my Mind.

He is writing not to tell his story to us, his heirs, but to 'deliver' his thoughts, to make his thoughts real before him, and in so doing, he says, my 'Reason began now to master my Despondency' (p. 65). And as this activity starts to settle Crusoe, to allow him to rationalise and to stabilise his condition, so he begins to write a journal – the journal, presumably, upon which the novel we are reading is based. Having 'gotten things in some Measure', he writes, by ordering his thoughts on paper, 'having settled my household stuff and Habitation', having built for himself a table and chair, he says, 'I began to keep my Journal, of which I shall here give you the Copy' (p. 69).

So far, one might think, so good. In line with Watt's account, Crusoe crafts for himself not only the material means of occupying a newly emerging form of sovereign state (habitation, table, chair), but also the discursive means with which we might picture it. The moment that Crusoe picks up his pen to write his journal with his salvaged ink is the moment that the novel begins to order a new world, arising from the shipwreck of the old. But no reader of this novel can fail to notice that the moment Crusoe begins to write this journal, the moment that the novel becomes interested in the means by which it comes to be written, is the moment at which everything starts to go wrong, when measure, order, and patient rationality are threatened with a kind of chaotic disorder, and a peculiar dark gulf opens between writing and being. The trouble starts just as the narrative prepares to shift from the first-person narration with which it starts to the diary form that it adopts when Crusoe hands the narrative over, as it were, to his journal. He did not keep a journal when he first got to the island, he says, because 'I was in too much hurry', and 'in too much Discomposure of Mind'. This is presumably why the opening of the novel comes to us in the form of extradiegetic narration, told retrospectively by a first-person narrator who is no longer present at the scenes he describes. He was in such a state on his first arrival, he says, 'that my journal would ha' been full of many dull things'. 'For Example', he goes on,

> I must have said thus. *Sept.* the 30th. After I got to the Shore and had escap'd drowning, instead of being thankful to God for my Deliverance, having first vomited with the great Quantity of salt Water which was gotten into my Stomach, and recovering my self a little, I ran about the Shore, wringing my Hands and beating my Head and Face, exclaiming at my Misery, and crying out, I was undone, undone, till tyr'd and faint I was forc'd to lye down on the Ground to repose, but durst not sleep for fear of being devour'd. (p. 69)

Fortunately, he suggests, he didn't write this entry because he was too busy wringing his hands and beating his own head. So, instead of the diaristic account that Crusoe didn't write, we fall back on the one that we were given twenty or so pages earlier, from the more balanced perspective of the extra-diegetic narrator who opens the novel. In this version, the first thing that Crusoe does when he arrives on shore is to make that very vote of thanks that he would have neglected had he written his journal entry at the time. 'I was now landed, and Safe on the Shore', he says, 'and began to look up and thank God that my Life was sav'd' (p. 46). Otherwise, though, the two accounts – the one that he doesn't write in the journal and the one that he has already given us – are quite similar. He gets on to shore, realises that he is 'undone', that he has no other 'Prospect' than 'that of perishing with hunger or being devour'd by wild Beasts', whereupon he is thrown into 'Agonies of Mind', so 'for a while I run around like a Mad-man' (p. 47). This is peculiar enough; the doubling of the account – that given first from a presumably reliable and naturalised narrative source, followed by the second account of what Crusoe might have written if he had described the event at the time – has the effect of throwing everything about the story so far into doubt. Did he thank God when he arrived on shore, or didn't he? Did he vomit great quantities of salt water, or didn't he? But things get much weirder when Crusoe as narrator hands the reins over to his own journal. 'I shall here give you the Copy', he says of the journal that he wrote on the island, though this might indeed mean that the narrative is 'full of dull things', because it means that 'in it will be told all these Particulars over again'. A new section is opened in the narrative, named 'the Journal', and we are cast right back, again, to 30 September 1659 – the day that Crusoe lands on the shore – to be told almost the same story that we have just been told, all over again. And inevitably the first entry, which describes Crusoe's arrival on the island, repeats the story of his despondent self-flagellation for the third time. The first entry of the journal tells of the morning that 'I came on shore on this dismal unfortunate island', and how, 'All the rest of the Day I spent in afflicting my self at the dismal Circumstances I was brought to' (p. 70).

This repetition has an extraordinary effect on the temporal and spatial unity of the novel. Where the opening sixty pages are told in a narrative fashion that assumes the authenticity of the tale, allowing for the creation of a robust reality effect (this is a 'just history of Fact', we are told, with 'no Appearance of Fiction in it' (p. 1)), the device of the journal entirely undermines this effect. It is not only that the three versions of Crusoe's arrival on the shore contain differences from one another, thus drawing attention to the fallibility of narration, the inescapability of 'fiction'; it is also that the stuttering repetition, the switching of narrative modes, the focus on Crusoe's act of recording and narrating, disrupts the flow of narrative time. Where the opening proceeds in a smooth temporal flow, recreating the experience of time passing on the island through the mimetic effects of narrative realism, the rather extraordinary decision to pass from first-person narration to a diary form draws our attention away from the narrated time – Crusoe's long inhabitation of the island – and towards the time of narration, the process of remembering and writing the tale itself. And if this is not destructive enough of the novel's realism, what is even more bizarre about this turn to the journal is that it entirely fails to sustain itself. Perhaps, one might think, Defoe draws attention to the journal in an attempt to *strengthen* the reality effect, to account as closely as he can for the process by which Crusoe remembers and records his time on the island; maybe so, but the single strangest thing about this novel is that the journal which offers itself as the primary source of the story does not manage fully to embed itself, or to achieve the lucid reality of the other objects on this island – the shovels and tables that Crowley suggests are rendered with such 'irreducible physicality'.

This strange unreality of Crusoe's island journal is produced in part by the failure of the narrative voice to remain securely housed within it. As we first enter into journal time, the narrative stays more or less within a diary format. The entry for 31 October, for example, reads 'The 31st. in the Morning I went out into the Island with my Gun to see for some Food, and discover the Country' (p. 71), and, on 3 November, 'I went out with my Gun and kill'd two Fowls like Ducks, which were very good Food. In the Afternoon went to work to make me a Table' (p. 71). This works fine, as the recording of Crusoe's actions, written by himself, in a journal some time more or less immediately after the event has taken place. The entry for 25 December, for example, gives us simply 'Rain all day' (p. 75) (what a Christmas!). But very quickly, the narrative voice finds the constraints of the journal too narrow, and starts first to move restlessly within them, and then to quietly exceed them altogether. So the entry for 1 January records how Crusoe found some goats in the middle of the island, and the following entry, for 2 January, records how 'Accordingly the next Day, I went out with my Dog, and set him upon the Goats' (p. 76). There is surely something wrong with this entry, something that does not quite obey the diary convention. Does a day recorded in a diary describe itself as 'the next day'? Is the idea not that one treats every day as a discrete event in its own right? The tendency to give not a day by day account of life on the island, but rather to tell the story over a larger time span, from a temporally mobile perspective located further in the future, surely belongs not to the diary format, but to the first-person narrative account with which we began? And sure enough, as we move from January, to April and May, the narrative voice frees itself for increasingly long stretches of time from anything like a diary mode, moving forward and backward in time for months and even years. Crusoe finds himself writing, in the entry that offers itself tenuously as 14 April, that 'I carefully sav'd the Ears of this Corn you may be sure in their season, which was about the end of *June*' – thus skipping forward by a couple of months from April to June, before reflecting that 'it was not until the 4th Year that I could allow myself the least grain of this corn to eat' – an enormous leap forward in time which returns the voice of the journal to exactly the same perspectival position as that of the first-person narrator. Crusoe and Defoe are aware of this tendency, because periodically Crusoe will interrupt himself in his free ranging narrative, to remind himself that he is supposed to be working in a diary format, supposed to be writing this not from some distant European perspective, but in the very sun and rain and wind of his remote island. After increasingly lengthy flights into the future, in which Crusoe reflects on the meaning of his life on the island, and the moral of the story as a whole, he will make the occasional half-hearted return to his journal: 'But to return to my journal', he says on 14 April; 'but I return to my journal', he says on 28 June; and then, on 4 July, 'But leaving this Part, I return to my journal', after which time the journal is never mentioned again and the voice quietly resumes the first-person narrative mode with which it began, as if it had never been interrupted.

Any attempt to understand the realism that Defoe develops in *Robinson Crusoe* has, I think, to respond to these fluctuations in narrative perspective. The novel is above all the story of how Crusoe shapes and rationalises the world in which he is cast away, and so the self-reflexive focus on the way that the narrative conceives of itself is an absolutely central part of this colonising process. The novel's obsessive concern with how it comes to be written is part of its philosophical examination of the ways in which words and ideas are attached to the things of the world, bound in a mutually transformative relationship with one another. The struggle to make for himself a home in writing, in his journal, is thus always represented as a mirror of the way that he struggles to make a home for himself on his island; making things out of wood is intimately entwined with the way that he makes things out of words. The construction of his burrow – his tunnelling into the rock to fashion for himself a cave in which 'I was compleatly fenc'd in, and fortify'd, as I thought, from all the World' (p. 59) – is similarly paired with the construction of an *account* of his homemaking in his journal. Throughout the novel, the process by which Crusoe shapes rock and wood is balanced against the process by which he applies words to the things he sees, and by which he attributes meaning to words and things, striving with his customary determination to force things into wordy shapes.

At the heart of this enterprise is Crusoe's growing religious belief, his gradual discovery of the centrality of God's will to his condition on the island, and by extension to the condition of the world more generally. He salvages from the wreck the pen and ink to write his journal, and at the same time he retrieves a copy of the Bible; these tools together, more than any other, offer him the means of crafting a dwelling place on the island. In the early years of his stay, Crusoe finds a gulf between word and thing, a gulf which he diagnoses as symptomatic of his Godless youth. His spiritual weakness means that word, sound and thing remain divorced from one another. On first opening the Bible, for example, Crusoe's eye falls upon the passage from the Psalms, which reads '*Call on me in the Day of Trouble, and I will deliver, and thou shalt glorify me*' (p. 94). These words, he remarks, 'were very apt to my case', but at this point in his spiritual development he cannot make them fit with his condition. 'As for being deliver'd', he thinks, 'the Word had no Sound, *as I may say*, to me' (p. 94). The word of God, at this point, remains a bodiless one to Crusoe, one with no materiality, which does not sound. And if the word of God has no sound, so too Crusoe finds that the only language that he does hear on the island in the early years of his stay contains no word, or no Word, remaining shrill and empty. At one point, on the return to his dwelling, Crusoe records that he is surprised by a voice that appears to be speaking to him, 'calling me by my Name several times', asking '*Robin, Robin, Robin Crusoe*, poor *Robin Crusoe*, where are you *Robin Crusoe*? Where are you? Where have you been?*'* (p. 142). This voice might sound like an echo of Crusoe's 'conscience', which earlier had upbraided him for his misspent youth – 'Methought', Crusoe remembers, his conscience 'spoke to me like a Voice', calling '*Wretch! Durst thou ask what thou hast done*' to deserve his banishment to the island (p. 92). This is what Dolar calls the 'internal voice of a moral injunction'.[12] But in this instance the voice is merely that of his parrot, who had heard Robinson use 'just such bemoaning Language', and 'had learn'd it so perfectly' (p. 142). This is not human language, not the language of God, but some kind of grotesque and empty animal copy, language reduced to babble, without any meaning or spirit. As Crusoe's conscience cannot marry word and thing, so God's word remains thingless, in the early years of Crusoe's stay, and the things of Crusoe's island remain wordless.

So, the writing of the journal – as part of Crusoe's Christian rationalisation of his condition, his 'Constant Study and serious Application of the Word of God' (p. 128) – is represented as the process whereby things and words are slowly, painfully brought together, the process by which, in Watt's terminology, Crusoe fashions the language with which to articulate an emergent capitalist modernity. In writing the journal, and in using writing to help him give shape to his growing consciousness of God – to his belief that there is a 'secret Hand of Providence governing the world' (p. 273) – Crusoe is reaching for a written form that could capture this immanent providential power, that could show us this power at work in the world. If Defoe is here producing a new kind of realism, one which diverts from the allegorical realism of Bunyan, then this is because he is aiming to demonstrate that the ideal, the divine, rests in the object itself, and that it is this discovery of the meaning of things in those things themselves that allows Crusoe to make for himself a rational existence out of his solitude. Where the word of God has no sound for Crusoe when he first lands on the island, where language is at first as empty of meaning and matter as the chattering of a parrot, his solitude allows Crusoe to 'gain a different Knowledge from what I had before', to 'entertain different Notions of things'. This knowledge comes not from instruction, or divine intervention, but from the slow realisation that the meaning of the world resides in the world itself, if only we can see the things of the world clearly, if only we can hear the resonance between word and thing. The meaning of 'Things', he reflects, 'occurr'd naturally to my Mind, upon my searching into them' (p. 220). The irreducible physicality of the objects Crusoe describes arises, then, because it is in such physicality that the meaning of the new world lies. But if this is the motive force behind the realism that Defoe crafts in *Robinson Crusoe*, it becomes all the more crucial to understand why the journal itself – upon whose reality the reality of all the objects on the island depends – is put under a kind of erasure. It is not simply that the novel fails to sustain the *voice* of the journal, in the way that I have described, so that the diaristic narration is strangely evacuated. It is also the case that the journal itself, as one of those objects that Crusoe takes such pleasure in describing and detailing, has a tendency to disappear, as if the very act of inscription is one which involves erasure, or is somehow fundamentally entwined with it. Crusoe notes, when he salvages his ink from the wreck, that he has only a short supply, and that furthermore, he 'could not make any Ink by any Means that I could devise' (p. 65). So he is forced to 'husband' his ink 'to the utmost', eeking it out as he eeks out his gunpowder, as if both substances – the fuel for pen and for sword – are the sustenance that allow him to carry on living; but, in tandem with the process by which the narrative voice gently frees itself from the journal mode, Crusoe acknowledges that his ink begins inevitably to run out, despite his utmost husbandry. After about a year on the island, Crusoe ruefully observes that 'My ink began to fail me, and so I contented myself to use it more sparingly and to write down only the most remarkable events of my life, without continuing a daily *memorandum* of other Things' (p. 104). And a little later he records how, in his desperation to maintain the journal that we are (sort of) reading, he began to dilute his ink. 'My Ink,' he writes, 'had been gone some time, all but a very little, which I eek'd out with Water a little and a little, till it was so pale it scarce left any Appearance of black upon the Paper' (p. 133).

The emergence of prose realism on Crusoe's island, then, the process by which he divines the convergence between words and things, is bound up with the disappearance of the very narrative procedures and apparatuses that enable it. Crusoe's development of a narrative voice – the narrative voice that is, in a sense, the birth of the modern novel – comes about not only through an act of inscription, but also through an act of erasure – or, more accurately, through an act of inscription that is also an act of erasure, that inscribes and erases at the same time. What

Defoe realises or intuits in *Robinson Crusoe* is that the establishment
of realism – of a kind of intimate narrative that captures the things of
the world in all their intractable physicality, their 'thereness' – requires
not only the building of a bond between word and thing, but also the
preservation of some kind of distance between them. It is as the ink of
Crusoe's journal runs out, leaving scarcely a mark upon the paper,
that he makes that transition that he longs for towards some kind of
accommodation with his God, because it is only through the articulation of some measured absence from self and from world that the kind
of narration that could articulate this accommodation can come into
being. As Crusoe presents us with the picture of his journal, as he
reveals to us the procedure by which he sits and inscribes the words
that we are reading at his roughly hewn table, he opens a radical gap
between the narrative he writes and the narrative we are reading, a gap
in which Crusoe himself as character and narrative agent is lost. 'To
return to my journal', he says – but we may ask, in the words of his
chattering parrot, where have you been Robin, where are you when you
are *not* in your journal? The realism that Defoe fashions means that we
have no answer to this question; when the narrative departs from the
journal format, when the ink runs out, Crusoe's mind drifts away from
itself, and from the words which constitute it, into some invisible
realm – the realm perhaps of novelistic narration. 'I wrote down only
the most remarkable events of my life', Crusoe writes in his journal, as
he tells us how he sets about preserving his ink. But with what ink are
these words written? A kind of invisible ink, perhaps; but if this is an
ink that leaves no trace, that does not belong to the world of objects
that Crusoe describes so lovingly to us, it is an invisible ink that is
absolutely crucial to the development of prose realism in the early
eighteenth century. It is only as a certain gap opens between word and
thing, only as narrative crafts a critical distance and freedom from the
world that it seeks to describe, that the world yields itself up to novelistic language. It is only as words evince an awareness of their own
incapacity to become one with that which they describe – only as a
terrible distance intervenes in the midst of the closest proximity, and a
certain invisibility glimmers in the most lucently visible of images –
that realism begins to exert a shaping force on the world before it.

III

Throughout the history of the novel, from Daniel Defoe to David Foster Wallace, it is possible to trace this difficult play between inscription and erasure as a constituent element of realism itself. It is not simply the case, I suggest, that a crisis occurs at some point in the history of the novel in which realism loses its capacity to represent the world – in which, in Costello's terms, the 'word-mirror is broken'. Rather, the history of realism itself is the history of an ongoing struggle between word and world, in which the capacity of the word to represent has always been fundamentally shaped by the resistance of the world to its mimetic power.

This struggle – what Jacques Rancière has called this 'complex set of relations between the visible and the invisible, the visible and speech, the said and the unsaid' (p. 93) – is there as Defoe sets out to craft a narrative form with which to give expression to western modernity; and one can see it developing and evolving as the modern novel grows from its birth in the early eighteenth century to the vigour of young adulthood in the works of the mid nineteenth century – the novels in which Smith's 'Balzac–Flaubert' model of lyrical realism reach their apogee. In the works that we might regard as representing the height of fictional realism – in the fiction of Zola, Flaubert and Balzac, of Tolstoy and Dostoevsky, of Hawthorne and Melville, of Thomas Hardy, Charles Dickens and perhaps pre-eminently George Eliot – we do not find a simple accord between word and thing, but rather an increasingly finely tuned dialectic between presence and absence, between limpid, luminous expression and a kind of darkness that, as Defoe discovers, is part of the expressive mechanism of narrative itself. While these novels reach for a kind of fullness of expression, one can find, at all times, a recurring fascination with the point at which the visible interacts with the invisible, and at which speech is woven into silence. Even as Eliot, in one of her most famous passages, suggests that the novelist's 'keen vision and feeling' might allow her to 'hear the grass grow and the squirrel's heart beat', the realist novel produces both an encounter with total seeing, and with a kind of failure of vision – an encounter, as Eliot puts it in that same passage, with that which lies 'on the other side of silence'.[13]

Take, for example, Eliot's reflections on the recuperative power
of the narrative voice – the element of realism, as I suggested in the last
chapter, that is most proper to the novel form. Throughout Eliot's
fiction, there is a rich investment in the voice both as the seat of being,
and as the medium in which the novel achieves its extraordinarily
deep seeing. Mirah, for example, the Jew who has become estranged
from her family at the opening of *Daniel Deronda*, comments on the
wonderful power of voice to enshrine memory and truth. She can
remember little of her mother and her brother Ezra, she says, but she
can 'remember my mother's voice calling, "Ezra!" and then his
answering from the distance, "Mother"' (p. 314). This answering
voice is all she knows of Ezra, but it is enough to convince her that
he is good and true ('I feel sure he is good', she says, 'I have always
taken comfort from that'), because the voice itself carries a kind of
truth, a kind of reality within it. As Mladen Dolar has argued, there is a
'long tradition' that associates ethics and the voice, a tradition that
turns around the inwardness of the 'voice of conscience'.[14] 'Is it not
wonderful', Mirah says, as she recalls the sound of her mother's voice,
and her brother's, 'how I remember voices better than anything else? I
think they must go deeper into us than other things' (p. 314).
Throughout *Deronda*, and across her fiction, Eliot draws on this capacity of narrative voice to penetrate character, and to capture the reality
of our being more profoundly than any other artistic medium. If Eliot
has a particular capacity to catch at the fine texture of thinking and
feeling, she does so by catching at the modulation of voice as it 'goes
deeper into us than other things'.

Indeed, at the heart of *Middlemarch* there is a recurrent and
insistent contrast between the capacity of visual arts to reflect reality,
and that of literary forms, those that speak to us with a voice rather
than come to us in the form of a picture. Dorothea's flirtation with the
artist Will Ladislaw begins unpropitiously with her refusal to accept
that his painting has any deep or meaningful relationship to the scenes
that he paints – 'I suppose', Dorothea says haughtily, 'there is some
relation between pictures and nature which I am too ignorant to feel'
(p. 79) – and both Dorothea and Ladislaw himself suggest that this
tinny reproduction of reality is nothing compared to the capacity of

fiction to hear the intimate movement of the mind itself as we experience the world, as we seek to make the world meaningful to us. When Ladislaw meets Dorothea for a second time – after she has married the elderly Mr Casaubon, and as the bride and groom are embarked on their gloomy honeymoon in Rome – the conversation again turns around the capacity of visual art to capture the real. Ladislaw and his painter friend Naumann come across Dorothea, standing in a painterly pose against the stone statue of 'Sleeping Ariadne' (see Figure 1), and their attention is drawn to the tense aesthetic relation between the beauty of the statue and that of the woman. Ariadne, the narrator says, 'lies in the marble voluptuousness of her beauty, the drapery folding around her with a petal-like ease and tenderness', and against this picture of frozen tenderness stands Dorothea herself, the 'breathing, blooming girl' (pp. 188–9) around which the narrative of *Middlemarch* turns. Naumann's painterly instincts are excited by this contrast. 'What do you think of that', he says, 'for a fine bit of antithesis?':

> There lies antique beauty, not corpse-like even in death, but arrested in the complete contentment of its sensuous perfection: and here stands beauty in its breathing life with the consciousness of Christian centuries in its bosom. (p. 189)

Naumann's response to this antithesis is a desire to make a picture of it, to commit this vibrating relation between antiquity and modernity, flesh and stone, life and death, to paint. But, against Naumann's visual imagination, Ladislaw, already influenced by Dorothea, asserts the primacy of language, and of narrative voice, in capturing breathing, blooming being. 'What is a portrait of a woman?' Ladislaw asks Naumann. 'Your painting and plastic are poor stuff after all. They perturb and dull conceptions instead of raising them.' In making and contemplating pictures, we are led to the frozen surface of things, rather than their fluid and mobile depths. 'The true seeing is within', Ladislaw insists, 'and painting stares at you with insistent imperfection.' To picture a woman in paint is to reduce her to 'mere coloured superficies', whereas 'language gives a fuller image', because it is able to capture 'movement and tone'. The final mark, for Ladislaw, of this superiority of language over paint is its capacity to

Figure 1: *Sleeping Ariadne;* in Vatican Museums

capture and reproduce voice, that manifestation of living, breathing language that goes deeper into us than other things, and that allows for us to see the within. 'This woman you have just seen', Ladislaw says to Naumann, 'how would you paint her voice pray? But her voice is much diviner than anything you have seen of her' (p. 191).

Voice, then, is the medium in which Eliot achieves her realism, a realism not of still surfaces but of moving depths. But if this is the case, if it is her control of voice, movement and tone that allows her to penetrate the real – or as Lydgate puts it in *Middlemarch*, to 'pierce' its 'obscurity' (p. 165) – it is also the case that this very penetrative power tends to destabilise and evacuate the writing, fully as much as it offers to ground it. Just as narrative voice in Dickens is composed of a compound of presence and absence, so the inward capacity of the voice in Eliot produces that same contradictory amalgam of inscription and erasure that we find in Defoe. The reason that 'language', for Ladislaw, 'is able to give a fuller image' is because it can catch at 'movement and tone', can follow the thinking mind in its rising and falling motion. Indeed, it is precisely this ability to see under the skin and into the intricate currents of the mind that the narrative of *Middlemarch* itself demonstrates, as the scene passes from Ladislaw and Naumann's observation of Dorothea, to the running motion of her inner thoughts as she stands by the statue of Ariadne, ruminating on her sad marriage to Casaubon. The narrative is able, in a classically Eliotian phrase, to follow Dorothea into the 'midst of her confused thought and passion', in order to witness the 'mental act' that is being born within her, just as it is 'struggling forth into clearness' (p. 192) as she stands, antithetically poised against the sleeping stone. This is the novel's capacity, as the narrator of *Daniel Deronda* puts it, to enter into the 'secret windings and recesses' of 'feeling' (p. 360). But in following movement and tone with such delicious subtlety, in tracing the process by which thought struggles to know itself or resolve itself into clarity, the narrative is brought, irresistibly, not against the stony foundation of thinking, but against its ethereal non-existence, its groundlessness. Voice can capture breathing being, Ladislaw says to Naumann, not in its essence but in its evanescence; or, perhaps better, it discovers that essence of being is itself evanescent. Voice finds the origin of vividly realised life in transition, change, difference. Naumann's painterly eye treats women as 'mere coloured superficies', but voice captures them in what Ladislaw calls their originary difference. 'There is a difference in their very breathing', he says, as he expands on the inability of paint to capture voice, 'they change from moment to moment' (p. 191). As the narrator of Thomas Hardy's novel *The Return of the Native* finds that it is the 'play of the features' that expresses character, rather than their fixity ('a face may make certain admissions by its outline', Hardy's narrator says, 'but it fully confesses only in its changes' (p. 56)), so Eliot's narrators find that the basis of being, the very ground of the breathing soul, lies in the experience of change. It is mercurial difference that instantiates characters, rather than any true fidelity that they bear to themselves.

This discovery of the reality of being not only in achieved, realised form, but also in the change and difference that seems to undermine or dissolve it, is an absolutely central and constitutive element of George Eliot's realism, and perhaps the element that most defines her aesthetic. Eliot's classically realist attention to character, her attempt to give the fullest expression to everybody, in their relation to everything, leads her continually to the underside of the real, to the 'other side of silence' (p. 194), as this underside, this other side, is what the real is made of. As the gentle curate Mr Farebrother says, late in *Middlemarch*, perhaps catching an echo of Ladislaw's earlier encounter with the sleeping Ariadne, 'character is not cut in marble – it is not something solid and unalterable. It is something living and changing, and may become diseased as our bodies do' (pp. 734–5). To realise that characters and bodies are constantly changing, and to seek to give expression to that realisation as part of a realist aesthetic, is to acknowledge that the world that we can see is only a fragment of reality, a partial, fleeting snapshot that is instantly obsolete. If Eliot's writing is motivated by a desire to make as much of the world visible to us as possible, then this desire always brings her into contact, in a beautiful and endlessly productive paradox, with darkness, with the invisible seams of difference and transition from which the visible itself is mined. As a result, the invisible is as much part of her picture of the world as the visible, and enters into a constant, difficult relationship with it. As Lydgate puts it in *Middlemarch*, to 'pierce the obscurity' of the real requires us to discover what he calls the 'invisible thoroughfares' that run through it, like capillaries (p. 165). Lydgate is rather scathing about what he calls 'indifferent drawing' and 'cheap narration'. These lesser art forms capture nothing, he thinks, but surfaces, whereas he is interested in 'the imagination that reveals subtle actions inaccessible by any sort of lens', that discovers the unseen processes that produce the real, rather than simply those that come to appearance. As Eliot has it in the epigraph to chapter 26 of *Daniel Deronda*, to produce a full account of the real is to respond to the fact that 'men, like planets, have both a visible and an invisible history'. If the 'narrator of human actions' is to 'do his work with the same completeness' as the astronomer, then he or she must learn, like the astronomer, to 'thread the darkness with strict deduction', to 'thread the hidden pathways of thought and feeling which lead up to every moment of action' (p. 139).

To understand Eliot's realism, then, is I think to recognise that her imagination takes her continually to that difficult point where the foundations of the real dissolve, and where narrative itself threatens to come undone, to unravel into the darkness that it seeks to make light. Her realism does not emerge from any secure sense that the real allows itself readily to take on word like form; on the contrary, her imagination comes from the interplay between the world that we can see, and those invisible forces that make history but that do not come to historical expression, those places that remain inaccessible even to her microscopic vision. And if Eliot gives a particularly sharp expression to this dialectic at the heart of prose realism, then it is the case, I think, that one can see this relationship – Rancière's 'complex set of relations' between 'the visible and the invisible', between 'the said and the unsaid' – at work throughout the history of the modern novel, from Defoe to Eliot to Kafka to Zadie Smith. Kafka's work, seen in the context of this long history, does not mark the abandonment of a realist project, but rather the intensification of it. When Kafka's strange, alienated creatures – the talking ape in 'Report to an Academy', the burrowing creature in his extraordinary story 'The Burrow' – enter into their peculiar darkness, in which the forces that hold us in place are suspended, they are not overthrowing the regime of realist expression that began with Defoe. Rather, they are living in and exploring that very gulf between narrative and the world, between words and what they mean, that Defoe opens as he sets out to write his journal in his disappearing ink. Indeed, there is perhaps no one that Kafka's creatures resemble more than Crusoe himself. When the protagonist of 'The Burrow' admires the dwelling place he has fashioned out of rock – when he lovingly beholds the underground 'castle' that he has 'wrested from the refractory soil with tooth and claw, with pounding and hammering blows' (145) – it is difficult not to see him as a descendent of Defoe's castaway, who laboriously fashions his own burrow, and who longs, with similar fervency, to be 'compleatly fenc'd in, and fortify'd, as I thought, from all the World'. In both Defoe and Kafka, realism does not simply involve making pictures of the world, but rather requires that we live in the bottomless gap between the word and the world, that is both the place from which we draw our understanding of the world, and the place into which such understanding continually collapses. Realism has always required us to face this risk, to encounter the endlessly shifting emptiness between words and what they mean, which makes of living itself a kind of recklessness. As those novelists who would extend this tradition now express their own dissatisfaction with realism, their own acknowledgement of its limits, it is this kind of risk at the heart of the realist tradition that they must acknowledge. The world has never been integrated, words have never agreed to stand up and be counted, each one proclaiming 'I mean what I mean'. It has been the purpose of the novel, throughout its history, to work with this refusal, and to make out of such refractory soil, such resistant materials, a kind of shelter, a kind of home. As we seek to refashion our understanding of realism now, as we try to determine which direction to travel along Zadie Smith's road, it is this rich sense of the difficulty and danger of realism, its beautiful disintegrated partiality, that we need to guide us.

PART II

Matter

3 The Novel Body

Oh! How immaterial are all materials! What things real are there, but imponderable thoughts?

Herman Melville, *Moby Dick*[1]

I began to perceive more deeply than it has ever yet been stated, the trembling immateriality, the mist-like transience, of this seemingly so solid body in which we walk attired.

Robert Louis Stevenson, *The Strange Case of Dr Jekyll and Mr Hyde*[2]

The opening of Samuel Beckett's excruciatingly condensed late work, *Worstward Ho*, gives perhaps the most succinct definition we have of what it is that the novel does. The narrator begins by instructing himself on what he must do in order to begin. 'Say a body', he says (commanding himself and obeying the command in the same breath). 'Say a body. Where none... A place. Where none. For the body. To be in.'[3]

These are the essentials of the fictional scenario. 'That', as the narrator puts it, 'at least'. In making fictions, we propose bodies taking up spaces, in the full knowledge that these bodies and these spaces do not exist. The defining feature of a novel body is its non-existence, its special talent for not being. As Theodor Adorno puts it, everything that happens in a novel, every element of its material texture, is defined and shaped by this fundamental property. 'Even an ordinary "was"', he writes, 'in a report of something that was not, acquires a new formal quality from the fact that it was not so'.[4] Or as Elizabeth Bowen writes, with a succinctness that echoes Beckett's, 'The novel lies, in saying something happened, that did not'.[5] To populate a fictional space with fictional bodies is to perform an act of engendering, of progeneration, which is also and at the same time the overseeing of a general extinction. The novelist imagines multitudes but he or she is also, to quote the French title of Beckett's late work *The Lost Ones*, a 'dépeupleur', a depeopler. As Thomas Bernhard's narrator says of his own narrative, in Bernhard's exquisitely comic novel *Extinction*, 'the sole purpose of my account will be to extinguish what it describes'.[6] Or, as Beckett's narrator Malone realises somewhat bemusedly, half way through his narrative, 'my notes have a curious tendency to annihilate all they purport to record'.[7] Or as the narrator of Tom McCarthy's recent novel *Remainder* discovers, the more grimly, the more assiduously we set about peopling the world of our fictions, the more insistently both people and world erase themselves. McCarthy's narrator takes a homeless person to a restaurant for dinner, fascinated by what he thinks is his earthy reality, his naked 'authenticity', and as he reaches across the table he knocks over a wine glass:

> The glass fell over and the wine sloshed out across the tablecloth. The tablecloth was white; the wine stained it deep red. The waiter came back over. He was ... she was young, with large dark glasses, an Italian woman. Large breasts. Small.
>
> The waiter leant across me as he took the tablecloth away. She took the table away too. There wasn't any table. The truth is, I've been making all this up.[8]

One might imagine that this act of implosion in McCarthy's novel should destroy it; surely such a total dismantling of the scene that the narrator is creating should have a calamitous impact on its reality effect. But what is striking here is that the destruction of the scenario, the de-peopling of the scene, does not break the rhythm of the writing at all, or even disrupt the 'authenticity' that the narrator effects to discover in the spectacle of poverty and statelessness that the homeless person represents to him. The wine stain on the tablecloth, the seeping of the red into the white, seems not a whit the less vivid for its sudden disappearance. The waiter too seems somehow to withstand the fluctuations in gender and body shape to which s/he is subjected. The unreality of the scene that the narrator describes is not the antidote to its realisation, but the very medium of its becoming. The narrator here is simply doing what novelists do – he is saying a body, where there is none, saying something happened, that did not.

As we move from the part I of this book to part II – from 'art' to 'matter', from 'form' to 'content' – it becomes necessary to ask what the aesthetic and political value of this kind of erasure is, and what we mean by 'content' or 'matter' under these conditions. What is a body in a novel, if it is also, quite categorically, *not* a body? What can the novelistic depiction of bodies tell us or help us to understand, if anything, about the condition of embodiment itself, about the material fact of living inside, and being oneself, a body? Another of Beckett's narrator's dwells on the peculiar purposelessness of a kind writing which is materialised in the throes of its own avowed immateriality. 'All I say cancels out', the narrator of *The Calmative* says, 'I'll have said nothing'.[9] What, we might ask, does it mean to 'say' nothing, to enclose nothingness in words, to 'weigh absence in a scale'?[10] It is hard not to hear in Beckett's career long fascination with the expression of non-expression an echo of Gustave Flaubert's earlier hymn to the beauty of a prose which might say nothing. 'What I find beautiful', Flaubert writes in an 1852 letter to Louise Colet,

> what I'd like to do, is a book about nothing, a book with no external attachment, which would hold together by the internal strength of its style, as the earth floats in the air unsupported, a book that would have almost no subject at all or at least one in which the subject would be almost invisible, if that were possible.[11]

For Beckett, as for McCarthy, for Bernhard, for Bowen, for Flaubert, the value of prose fiction, and of prose style, is perhaps found in the capacity not to depict bodies but to erase them, to reveal their non-being. 'The most beautiful works', Flaubert writes, 'are those with the least matter [matière]; the more expression coincides with thought, the closer the word adheres to it and vanishes into it, the more beautiful it is'.[12] Fiction, or at least beautiful fiction, is not a means of encountering, representing or exploring the body, but a means of escaping from it, a means of 'vanishing' into 'thought'.

This account, of course, might suggest that the attempt to find bodies in novels is a rather fatuous task, or that to shift our focus from 'art' to 'matter' is rather perversely to refuse to see that literature is precisely the place where matter itself disappears. But what I want to argue here is that the relationship between fiction and matter – even in those writers who have sought most strenuously to rid their imagination of the polluting presence of 'stuff' – is absolutely central, both to our understanding of fiction and to our understanding of matter. It is very difficult, I think, to conceive of matter without fiction. It is perhaps only when one tells a story about the world that it comes into any sort of perceptibility, even if the process of storytelling itself admits, necessarily, of a degree of falsehood, a degree of invention (thus erasing in the very act of inscribing). But it is equally impossible to conceive of fiction without matter. As Flaubert acknowledges, even in the midst of his eulogy to nothingness, fiction itself is bound up with matter – it seeks to represent matter, and is itself matter. Despite his infatuation with the 'loftiness of the idea', he writes in that same letter to Colet, he is also a materialist, who 'digs and burrows into the truth as far as he can, who loves to represent the little detail as powerfully as any other kind, who would like to make you feel almost *materially* [*matériellement*] the objects he reproduces' (p. 30; p. 131 (emphasis in original)). As James Wood has argued, Flaubert does not simply empty his fictions of matter, but conducts a kind of contradictory struggle between matter and literary nothingness. He seeks, Wood writes, 'to write on the one hand fiction that is densely detailed, densely involved with matter, and on the other hand fiction without matter, because his style refuses the pull of matter, asserts itself over matter'.[13] To understand the value of the novel, to understand the role the novel has played in making the world and our own bodies inhabitable for us, it is I think necessary to attend to this play between fiction and matter, this capacity of fiction on the one hand to capture matter, and on the other hand to evacuate it – this capacity to say that there is a body, while saying also that there is none.

This question of the relationship between 'matter' and 'nothingness' is central, then, to any understanding of the means by which novels imagine being; but I think that the question takes on a certain urgency at this point in the history of critical and political thought, when our conception of the relationship between ideas and material is entering into a state of transition. The passage from Flaubert to Beckett is one that has seen the steady dematerialisation of our cultural referents, not only of our bodies but also of the physical environments in which we live. The historical tendency of modernity has been towards disappearance, towards the transformation of material into ideas, or what is now called 'information'. This tendency can be seen across the spectrum of cultural experience, from the virtualisation of capital, to the aesthetics of modernism and postmodernism, to the politics of postcolonialism, and thirdwave and postfeminism. The development of literary and critical thought over the last century and more has seen a powerful confluence of late-stage capitalism with revolutionary information technologies with modernist and postmodernist aesthetics – a confluence that has produced a context within which the immateriality of novel bodies has come to stand in for a more general groundlessness to contemporary being. If a novel says a body when there is none, this is not a failure of its representational duty, but a sign of its special access to a truth about the non-existence of our bodies. Novel bodies speak acutely of our condition, because we, like them, are made up, printed out. If, as Judith Butler puts it in *Bodies That Matter*, 'discourse materializes a set of *effects*',[14] then the novel is perhaps the exemplary form in which we might test this capacity for discourse to realise itself, whilst always insisting upon its immateriality, its freedom from Flaubert's 'external attachments'. The shape shifting, gender indeterminate waiter in McCarthy's *Remainder* is perhaps not a mark of that novel's abandonment of novelistic protocol, its weary relinquishment of the trappings of storytelling propriety; it is perhaps instead a late example of a novelistic capacity to simultaneously 'say' and 'unsay' the body that has been a central concern of the novel since at least Flaubert. From the extraordinarily unstable picture of the gendered body that we find in Virginia Woolf's *Orlando*, or Radclyffe Hall's *Well of Loneliness*, or Djuna Barnes *Nightwood*, to the ambiguities around sexuality and race in Nella Larsen's *Passing* and Ralph Ellison's *Invisible Man*, to the experiments with fictional identities in Angela Carter's *The Passion of New Eve*, J.G. Ballard's *The Atrocity Exhibition* and Rushdie's *Midnight's Children* and *Satanic Verses*, the novel has found in the very fictionality of the body – its capacity for Flaubertian invisibility – a means of exploring and intervening in the political forces that produce our life-worlds.

But, if this has been the dominant tendency in the west throughout the second half of the last century, we have entered a period over the last two decades or so in which the balance between idealist and materialist elements in the culture has tilted towards a new materialism. Major shifts in the way that global culture is produced, combined with a dramatic waning of postmodernism as a 'cultural dominant', have broken the spell that made our bodies invisible to us, and as a result we are seeing the re-emergence of a kind of plastic substrate to being, the reassertion of the oozing stuff of life. In the west there has been what Steven Connor has called a 'thingly turn, a *neue Sachlichkeit*, a *nouveau chosisme*'. 'For at least two decades', Connor wrote in 2010, 'there has been a slow, incremental, but by now immense stirring of things'.[15] With tectonic shifts in the global distribution of capital, with the emergence of China and India as world economic powers, with massive transformations in the global balance of power after 9/11, with the decline of US imperial power, and, most dramatically, with the growing urgency of eco-catastrophe as the horizon of all addresses to the future, the docility of things, their willingness to appear as the disposable wrappings of thought, has come to an end. It was as the west reached the height of its power in the wake of the cold-war, as history appeared to be drawing to a close, as western capital appeared to be synonymous with the very virtual-global environments we inhabited, that bodies receded to the point of invisibility, becoming, in Donna Haraway's memorable phrase, 'nothing but signals, electromagnetic waves'.[16] But as western states and western markets begin to lose their world-shaping power at the dawn of the new century, we see what Alain Badiou has recently called the 'rebirth of history'[17] and, with it, the re-appearance of the stubbornly material grounds upon which discursive processes are played out. A group of thinkers have come to prominence, such as Giorgio Agamben, Jacques Rancière and Alain Badiou, who have sought to formulate the means by which state power and cultural discourses operate upon biological bodies, without reducing bodies to the simple expression of such power or such discursivity. And the work of thinkers such as Judith Butler has itself taken a more materialist turn, in response to a general and urgent need to reassess the ways in which ideological, discursive and historical forces operate upon bodies and environments which suddenly seem more real to us, just as they seem more dangerously precarious. As Judith Butler recognises in her 2004 work *Precarious Life*, life returns in its biological physicality as a result of our recognition of its new precarity.

With these shifts, and in the churned wake of a giant thingly turn in what corporate executives call our 'direction of travel', it is possible to see that our understanding of the novel body is entering too into a transformative period, in which we are led to rebalance the material against the ideal and to reassert Flaubert's dense 'involvement with matter' against his infatuation with nothingness and invisibility. The prevailing critical mood of the later twentieth century made it very easy to attend to the abstraction of prose fiction, to its capacity to reshape and reimagine bodies which always declared their non-existence; but it was very much more difficult, under those conditions, to account for the materiality of novel bodies, their stickiness, the sense that bodies couched in words might have some kind of connection with bodies couched in matter. Material bodies could readily appear to be like language; but it was not so easy to see it the other way around, to imagine that words might be like bodies, or share the properties of bodies. But, in terms of the critical and political context now emerging, it becomes possible, even necessary, to re-see the materiality of novel bodies, to retrace a history of the embodied fictional imagination, which has always been there, but which has been harder to discern under postmodern conditions. If the tradition that I have been sketching here – that runs from Flaubert through Woolf to Beckett, Bernhard and McCarthy – might lend itself quite readily to the apparent disappearance of bodies in language, then it is possible to trace another literary tradition that suggests a more or less opposite attitude to the relation between fiction and the body – one that sees the novel as the art form that is the most attentive to the material weight of the body, rather than that in which the body tends to disappear. As Elaine Scarry has influentially suggested, language is not simply the discursive counterpoint to material, but is also 'capable of registering in its own contours the weight of the material world';[18] the history of the novel is, in one sense, a long exploration of this capacity. From the laborious fashioning of the relationship between words and things that I traced in the last chapter in Defoe's *Crusoe*, through the explorations of embodied being in Laurence Sterne's *Tristram Shandy* and Sarah Scott's *Millenium Hall*, to the great Russian, English, French and American novels of the nineteenth century, the novel has been the place where the body has been most fully explored – where the condition of living inside a body is encountered more intimately, more molecularly, than anything that could be presented on stage, on canvas or on celluloid.

It is perhaps in the weighted, Rabelaisian language of Jonathan Swift, particularly in his masterpiece *Gulliver's Travels*, that this capacity for fiction to take on the bulk of matter is at its most insistently embodied. When Gulliver travels to Lilliput and then to Brobdingnag, Swift gives us a compelling account both of the sheer physicality of the body, and of our attempts to capture it in language, to fashion some kind of discursive form that might enable us to tame or master its grotesqueries. As Gulliver arrives at the tiny shore of Lilliput, Swift's language immediately conveys the suddenly huge proportions of Gulliver's body, registering the weight of the body, as Scarry might put it, in its own contours. Even before Gulliver has met any of the diminutive inhabitants of Lilliput, just as he swims ashore from his shipwreck, the language evokes his imminent giantism. As he reaches for the sea bottom in his approach to land, he writes that 'I often let my Legs drop',[19] and in that short phrase Gulliver's body already begins to swell, to extend under his own gaze like Lewis Carroll's Alice when she drinks one of her metamorphic potions. The peculiar lack of agency that the phrase suggests – Gulliver does move his own legs but lets them fall under their own massive weight – is a foretaste of the strange bodily discomposure that comes over Gulliver, as his comparison to the tiny Lilliputians makes his body feel vast, uncontainable, suddenly remote from the stories that he might tell himself about it. As his visit to Lilliput unfolds, this alienation only becomes more marked. Gulliver recounts how the Lilliputian king 'commanded that several Ladders should be applied to my Sides, on which above an hundred of the Inhabitants mounted' (p. 9), again expressing that strange lack of ownership, that strange distance from his 'Sides', as if he were a building or a hill (or a 'man mountain'). And when he travels to Brobdingnag, this situation is cruelly reversed, allowing him to see with horror the same gruesome, untenanted materiality of the body that he himself experienced in Lilliput. He tells of his meeting with a 'Woman with a Cancer in her Breast, swelled to a monstrous Size, full of Holes, in two or three of which I could easily have crept, and covered my whole Body' (p. 101). Now, in one sense such gruesome depictions of the magnified body might suggest not so much the capacity of language to master matter, but rather its failure to accommodate the brute thereness of biological being, its failure to transform bare life into subjectivity or coherent identity. As the frames through which we see the world shift, in the course of England's imperial domination of the globe in the early eighteenth century, the body becomes difficult to master, unresponsive to the claims of the sovereign subject. The strange porousness of the giant, cancerous body – the sense that the skin is not a tight, sealed boundary that encloses the body, but a grotesquely open field through which other bodies might freely pass – signifies this rather horrific unruliness of bodily material. But it is in his very performance of the failure of language to master unregulated biological material that Swift most effectively captures the materiality of the body. Where Virginia Woolf later explores the triumph of consciousness over matter – opening the boundaries of the self by allowing for the free passage of *thought* from one person to another – Swift explores the opposite movement: the triumph of matter over consciousness. Gulliver's nauseated regard of the Brobdingnagian woman's breast allows him to imagine crawling into the most intimate space of the other, but this is a bodily congress that spells the absolute failure of all forms of social or spiritual communication. There is no erotic, maternal or aesthetic rhetoric that could shape this breast, that could make it readable to Gulliver, or meaningfully relatable to his own body. Rather, the picture of the body in *Gulliver's Travels* is one in which the body becomes so present, so *there*, as to overwhelm discursive structures, to crowd them out with the stuff of being.

It is perhaps this kind of tradition of material embodiment that D.H. Lawrence evokes in his essay from 1925, punningly entitled

'Why the Novel Matters'. In this essay, Lawrence suggests a picture of
the novel body that appears starkly opposed to the disappearing body
that we find in Beckett, Bernhard and McCarthy, the body that exists
only in the process of its own erasure. For Lawrence, it is the novel,
and the novel supremely, that is able to capture the body in its materiality, in its aliveness. 'The novel', Lawrence writes, 'is the book of
life'.[20] If Swift struggles to maintain a picture of Gulliver as an
integrated subject, if the sheer materiality of existence threatens in
Gulliver's Travels to overwhelm the sovereign being who would
declare ownership of the body, then for Lawrence this is because the
novel itself is attuned to the primacy of vibrating, trembling living
over the pale cast of thought. In an attack on the idealist tradition I
traced earlier in this chapter – in a broadside against what he calls
'these damned philosophers' – he insists that the novel *knows* life, and
the immanent, vibrating self-presence of life, in a way that no other
discursive form can. The novel demonstrates that the body should not
and cannot be subservient to some notion of consciousness or soul or
mind – that these vapid constructions could never contain or stand in
for the quick energy of living flesh. To imagine that the body is some
sort of removable addition or attachment to the soul, he says, is 'a
funny sort of superstition'. 'Why should I look at my hand', he goes on,

> as it so cleverly writes these words, and decide that it is a mere nothing
> compared to the mind that directs it? My hand is alive, it flickers with a mind
> of its own. My hand, as it writes these words, slips gaily along, jumps like a
> grasshopper to dot an i, feels the table rather cold, gets a little bored if I write
> too long, has its own rudiments of thought, and is just as much *me* as is my
> brain, my mind, or my soul. Why should I imagine that there is a *me* which is
> more *me* than my hand is? (p. 193)

The attentiveness to the presence of the body – that material attentiveness that Lawrence says is the particular province of the novel –
produces that same, odd disintegration of the self that we find in
Gulliver. Here, Lawrence's consciousness of the being of his hand as
it writes the essay we are reading leads him to express a certain
alienation from his own text. 'My hand' writes the text, he says, it
'slips gaily along'; but of course he claims too that 'I' write the text,
and in fact the 'I' that writes might come into some disagreement with

the 'hand' that writes, the hand that might get a little bored and fidgety having to transcribe Lawrence's tedious sermonising. But Lawrence insists in this essay that this very alienation, this crowded variousness of the self, is the mark of the novel's wholeness, its capacity to capture being in its completeness. It is only the novel, he writes, that can capture life in all its elements, in its mental and physical extensions, its erotic and intellectual and elemental cravings. 'I absolutely flatly deny', he writes, 'that I am a soul, or a body, or a mind, or an intelligence, or a brain, or a nervous system, or a bunch of glands, or any of the rest of these bits of me' (p. 195). What he feels himself to be is whole and various, and, he says, it is the novel that can capture this wholeness, even by giving expression to its conflictedness, its internal incompatibility. The philosopher will regard being as pure thought, a 'tremulation on the ether, like a radio message' (p. 194). The scientist 'puts under the microscope a bit of dead me, and calls it me' (p. 195). But it is only the novel that can 'make the whole man alive tremble'. 'The saint, the scientist, the philosopher and the poet', he writes, 'are all great masters of different bits of man-alive', but 'only in the novel are *all* things given full play' (p. 198).

This close relation between the novel and biological life, which one can find both in Lawrence and in Swift, is perhaps one of those elements of materiality that has been difficult to articulate in recent times, but which is now beginning to call for a new critical attention. If it is the case, as Elaine Scarry and Perry Anderson have argued, that the later twentieth century saw a new attention to the relationship between literature and the body – a 'sudden zest, a new appetite for the concrete'[21] that is a close relation of Steven Connor's 'thingly turn' – then the history of the novel, and of the novel body, might offer a rich resource on which to draw in an attempt to understand how bodily things make an imprint or an impression on wordy things, things made in words. To think about novel bodies today, I suggest, is to attend to this impression, to develop a new means of approaching that peculiar disappearing intersection between bodies living in the world, and bodies as we make them inhabitable or thinkable by means of narrative – narrative as a kind of binding mechanism that secures our tenancy within our own living tissue. But if this is so – if the critical forces operating on us today require us to rethink this pressure that materiality exerts upon language and upon consciousness – it is also crucial that our re-seeing of this material history does not overcompensate in the other direction – does not make light of that talent for non-existence that is so critical a feature of the novel body. As Elizabeth Bowen very beautifully puts it, 'without their indistinctness things do not exist'.[22] Lawrence's insistence on the wholeness and self-sufficiency of the body can seem, to those of us accustomed to a late twentieth-century insistence on the virtuality of the culture and the discursive or simulacral nature of political life, peculiarly brutish and reactionary. The revolutionary energy of many developments in feminist politics, and identity politics more generally, has grown from a rejection of the essential nature of the body, an insistence that bodies are never entire, never sufficient to themselves, but are fashioned in part out of Bowen's indistinctness, out of their radical incompleteness. It is the doctrine that bodies are meaningful in themselves – that bodies are intrinsically raced, gendered, classed – that has allowed for every political outrage, from slavery to Nazism to generations upon generations of the oppression of women. To re-read novel bodies now is not, under any circumstances, to return to these prior certainties about bodily integrity. But it is, I think, to recognise that discursive constructs are always involved in a difficult relationship with the materiality that they work upon, and that in some ways constitute them, and that the novel body itself is a difficult, contradictory, partial result of that ongoing struggle between language and the material conditions of existence.

Indeed, one way of tracing this contradiction between art and matter is to attend to an obsession with the representation of hands that stretches across the history of the novel, an obsession that Lawrence is knowingly drawing on in his 1925 essay. For Lawrence, to capture his hand in narrative is to encounter and transcribe the sealed boundaries of the body, to distinguish between what is a living part of the self and what is, to use Flaubert's terminology, an 'external attachment'. 'As far as I'm concerned', Lawrence writes, 'Me alive ends at my finger tips' (p. 193). His hand holds a pen, a kind of prosthetic supplement which allows him to ink the words that his hand forms onto the page; but 'of course', he says, 'my pen isn't alive at all. My pen *isn't me* alive'. 'Every tiny bit of my hands is alive', he goes on, 'every little freckle and hair and fold of skin' (p. 193), and this liveness is to be absolutely opposed to any external, non-living attachments, either philosophical or material, that might be added to the hand, to help it fulfil its function or to allow us to conceive an idea of its function. This is what the novel as 'the book of life' allows us to experience and represent. But, as Lawrence knows, the novel is driven by an encounter with the hand not simply as the guarantor of the self-identical, enclosed subject, but as the sign of bodily extension in which the nature of the relationship between writing, body and world is at its most open. From Defoe's struggle to find the 'secret Hand of Providence' (p. 273) at work in the world, to the struggle with what she calls the 'dead hand' in Eliot's *Middlemarch* and *Daniel Deronda*, to the encounter with the monstrous hand in Robert Louis Stevenson's *Dr Jekyll and Mr Hyde*, to the murderous hand in Émile Zola's *Thérèse Raquin*, to the sickeningly alienated hand in Jean Paul Sartre's *Nausea*, to the automated hands that we find in Samuel Beckett and Elizabeth Bowen, the novel hand operates at that strange and disturbing boundary between self and world, between art and matter. It occurs so insistently in the novel imagination in part because it seems so richly to signify selfhood. As in the twisted plot of *Jekyll and Hyde*, the hand is a metonym for the signature – the coming together of the written word and persistent self-identity – and the hand offers itself by extension as a seat of being, as central to the experience of one's identity as the heart or the head. It is the hand which most richly evokes our biopolitical extension into the world, our reaching from inner to outer, from self to other. It is the hand that is the privileged vehicle of touch. But even as it appears to be the guarantor of identity, the sign and signature of the living self at work in the world, the hand threatens to defy the cohering power of the narrated self, to move beyond it, to exhibit extraneousness from self and from writing. From the 'lean, corded, knuckly hand' of Mr Hyde[23] to the peculiarly autonomous, 'unexploring' hands at the heart of Elizabeth Bowen's *The House in Paris*,[24] the hand has exercised a kind of resistance to the authority of writing, a kind of fleshy unruliness. As it recurs throughout the novel, then, the hand lives out the struggle of fiction to control matter: the novel seeks (as in Escher's famous drawing) to contain the writing hand within its own economy of signs, to make it part of that narrative that posits a body where there is none; but in its encounter with the hand, the novel is brought repeatedly against a bodily supplement, hand as flesh which exceeds the novel's economy, and which the novel cannot do without. We imagine that the writing hand is ours, that the hand is doing our bidding as it inscribes our words onto the page; but, as Beckett's Malone knows, as the narrator of Lawrence's essay knows, the hand extends into a world of plastic stuff that no writing can overcome. As Malone says, as he writes the narrative we are reading, 'my little finger glides before the pencil across the page and gives warning, falling over the edge, that the end of the line is near' (p. 207).

There is possibly nowhere in the history of the novel where this contradiction between writing and biomatter is present in a more maximal state than in Herman Melville's extraordinary novel *Moby Dick*. It is hard to imagine that there is a novel, or indeed any other art object, that more fully reproduces the materiality of embodied being. The whale, that animated mountain of fleshy life that Melville and Shakespeare call 'the sovereignest thing on earth',[25] is the very manifestation, for Melville, of material life. The whole novel – itself massive, cetaceous – thrills with the enormity of the whale, its primordial, unknowable, unimaginable vastness. What Melville attempts in *Moby Dick*, above all else, is to craft a language that might capture this vastness within its own 'contours', that might somehow fuse with the enormity of the whale, to provide a language that is made of mass, of flesh, of weighty, coursing life. To write of the whale, Ishmael says, is to 'stagger under the weightiest words of the dictionary' (p. 406). It is to plunge one's very hands into the stuff of being, to immerse oneself in alienly living flesh, just as Swift's Gulliver imagines crawling into the giant mass of the Brobdingnagian woman's breast. It is to enter at once into the depths of language and into the depths of the palpable, numinous world. 'I have swam through libraries and sailed through oceans', Ishmael says; 'I have had to do with whales with these visible hands' (p. 118). In order to sound the depth of the whale, he has sought to 'grope down into the bottom of the sea after them; to have one's hands among the unspeakable foundations, ribs, and very pelvis of the world' (p. 118). To write of the corporeal whale, whose 'liver was two cart loads' (p. xliv), whose breath 'is frequently attended with such an unsupportable smell, as to bring on a disorder of the brain' (p. xlvi), is to cast oneself into a kind of being that is as materially present to itself as that life that Lawrence imagines when he see his own living hand. Indeed, it allows Ishmael to imagine a kind of universal life, a kind of being of the mingled flesh that would free us altogether from the turmoil and torment of thinking, of discriminating one thing from another, one person from another, one species from another. Ishmael gives us an account of the process whereby the whalemen squeeze the oil of a freshly killed sperm whale, in order to massage lumps that have formed in the cooling 'sperm' back into a clear fluid. In squeezing the sperm in this way, Ishmael suggests, his hands are immersed literally rather than metaphorically in the material being of the whale; and, in entering so intimately into the body of the whale, Ishmael encounters a kind of intense bonding with the hands of his comrades, a kind of homoerotic fusion with whale and fellow man. He squeezed the sperm, he says, 'all the morning long':

> I squeezed that sperm until I almost melted into it; I squeezed that sperm till a sort of insanity came over me; and I found myself unwittingly squeezing my co-laborers' hands in it, mistaking their hands for the gentle globules. (p. 373)

The meeting of hands here, in the melted stuff of the whale, allows for a glimpse of a utopian homosociality, a seamless biological union with our 'fellow beings' in which we 'no longer cherish any social acerbities, or know the slightest ill-humor or envy'. 'Come', Ishmael says, as he plunges his hands into the warm sperm of the whale, 'let us squeeze hands all round; nay, let us squeeze ourselves into each other; let us squeeze ourselves universally into the very milk and sperm of kindness' (p. 373).

The struggle to write the whale in *Moby Dick*, then, is in part this attempt to make language into a body, a collective body in which we are all squeezed into each other, as Gulliver imagines himself squeezing into a giant cancerous breast. But, if *Moby Dick* might be the work in which this convergence of language with material is the most consummate, in which words become as weighty as that which they signify, it is also the case that this novel performs the opposite tendency that I have been discussing, the antithetical impulse of the contradiction between matter and nothingness. Indeed, to some degree this urge towards the inexpressible is a simple, if paradoxical, *effect* of its materiality. As language tends to give way before the enormity of bodily being in Swift's *Gulliver*, so in Melville there is a recurrent tendency for language to fail when faced with the enormity of the whale's corpulent mass. The more Melville's language takes on the bulk of the whale's being, the more inarticulate it becomes, as matter overwhelms thought and makes language fall silent. As Patrick McGrath puts it, 'whatever the truth of the whale, clearly language cannot contain it, the reality of any phenomenon for Melville being deeper than language, deeper even than the appearance of the thing'.[26] As Melville's novel reaches for the reality of things, as Ishmael plunges his word hands into 'the foundations, ribs, and very pelvis of the world', he finds that these things remain 'unspeakable' and only yield themselves to him on condition of that unspeakability. The magnitude of the whale proofs it against capture in nets or in language. 'As yet', Ishmael says, 'he lives not complete in any literature'. 'His is an unwritten life', and to write the whale is to encounter this unwriting, a kind of unknowing that attends material things in their materiality. 'Dissect him how I may', Ishmael admits, 'I but go skin deep; I know him not, and never will' (p. 339). But if the inexpressible in *Moby Dick* is a symptom of this passion for the material, a peculiar proof of the novel's fidelity to the unwritten whale, it is also more than this; it is also an actual, purposive urge towards vanishing, towards disappearance, that is as central to Melville's realism as it is to George Eliot's. Melville's novel thrills with a Flaubertian desire to vanish into thought that is just as passionate as its involvement with matter, even as it paradoxically emerges from it. The 'visible hands' with which Ishmael reaches into the foundations of the world, the spermy hands with which he squeezes the hands of his fellow men, are paired with the shade of an invisible hand that never stops haunting this novel, and that attends all material measure with a kind of spectral counter-measure, all touch with an invisible counter-touch. At the opening of the novel, Ishmael tells the story of a childhood nightmare in which he dreamt that he was visited by a 'nameless, unimaginable, silent form or phantom', whose 'supernatural hand seemed placed in mine'. 'I lay there', Ishmael remembers, 'frozen with the most awful fears, not daring to drag my hand away' (p. 23). He never discovers what this hand was, or to whom it belongs – 'to this very hour', he writes, 'I often puzzle myself with it' (p. 24) – but its presence can be felt throughout *Moby Dick* as the weightless spiritual counterweight to matter, the moving presence of the idea within the thing, the idea of the hand that animates the hand, never quite becoming one with it, never achieving that self-sameness, that idea perfectly clad in flesh, that Lawrence reaches for in 'Why the Novel Matters'.

It is in the awful figure of Ahab, the monomaniacal sea captain madly bent on the vengeful murder of Moby Dick, that this struggle between matter and idea reaches its most intense expression. Ahab, seen in a certain light, is the most material of beings. He is described repeatedly as inanimate matter rather than flesh – as wood, or ivory, or bone. 'His whole high, broad form', Ishmael says, 'seemed made of solid bronze, and shaped in an unalterable mould, Like Cellini's cast Perseus' (p. 108). Indeed, in his very materiality, he shares something with the whale itself, the creature who is his deadly foe. His first encounter with Moby Dick cost Ahab his leg, and the prosthetic leg that he wears throughout the novel is fashioned from the jawbone of the sperm whale, as if, in 'dismasting' Ahab, Moby Dick has annexed him, transformed him into whale. Not only his whalebone leg, but his whole patchwork body suggests this strange amalgamation of man and fish. Moby Dick is known by his 'prominent features', a 'peculiar snow-white wrinkled forehead, and a high, pyramidical white hump' (p. 163), and Ahab himself is described repeatedly as having a 'wrinkled brow' (p. 177); he is also 'bowed and humped' (p. 480), his prosthetic leg is also 'snow-white' (p. 422), and like the whale he has a white seam running through his body, a 'lividly whitish' (p. 108) birthmark that streaks through him like lightening through a blasted tree. It is as if the intense struggle with the whale has overtaken his physical form, so Ahab feels barely able to occupy his body, barely able to animate it. Like the body of the whale, or the body of the giant Gulliver, Ahab's body is so dense, so material, that is has become unresponsive to the claim of thinking, the claim of idea or spirit. As the 'innermost life' (p. 258) of the whale is secreted somewhere beneath its folds and folds of biological material, so buried in itself that it is barely discernible as the animating principle behind all that massively moving matter, so Ahab's body seems devoid of soul, a clockwork mechanism that owes its graven materiality to its remoteness from the life that pilots it.

But if the novel presents Ahab's prosthetic body as inanimate material, this is not, in any sense, a mark of the triumph of matter over spirit; Ahab's partaking of the being of the whale bears no resemblance to the utopian devotion to the mingled, hybrid flesh that Ishmael feels as he squeezes the spermy hands of his comrades. Rather, Ahab's insensate flesh owes its solidity to his absolute commitment to spirit over matter – to his insane obsession with a single, pulsing, beating thought: his hatred of the whale. Ahab's hatred is such that his material form cannot contain it, just as the dissolving body of Dr Jekyll cannot 'contain the raging energies' of Mr Hyde (p. 85). His body goes dead and numb, becomes thing-like, as his tormented brain beats against the confines of his skull, seeking to dissolve itself into a pure, uncontaminated lust for vengeance. Ahab shatters his whale-bone leg late in the novel, in another of his skirmishes with the white whale, but, he insists, to injure his body – either his prosthetic body or his fleshy body – has no effect on his true being, the life that he has in his tormented, vengeful mind. The bone that is made of whale, he says, is no more *him* than the bone that is made of Ahab. Lawrence writes that the hand that he sees before him 'is just as much *me* as is my brain, my mind, or my soul'; Ahab insists – demands – that the opposite is the case, that his hand, his leg, has no claim on his soul, which has no material component, which vanishes into pure thought. His leg is 'all splintered to pieces', Ahab cries, 'but even with a broken bone, old Ahab is untouched'. To lose a prosthetic leg, to lose a living leg, makes no dent in him, he says. 'I account no living bone of mine one jot more me, than this dead one that's lost' (p. 496). There is nothing, no body, no whale, no enemy, that 'can so much as graze old Ahab in his own proper and inaccessible being' (p. 495). Not only his body, but the material world itself seems to Ahab a prosthetic contrivance, some 'fleshy tabernacle' in which 'the soul' is 'glued', a clattering, blubbery machinery that pins us down, that holds us inside the bleeding folds of life, but which the power of impassioned thought can resolve into a dew. 'All visible objects', he insists, 'are but as pasteboard masks' (p. 145), the disposable trappings in which ideas present themselves or dissemble themselves to us. Behind that 'unreasoning mask', Ahab goes on, 'some unknown but still reasoning thing puts forth the moulding of its features', and it is his task, as he sees it, to break through that mask, to tear asunder the material bodies in which we are imprisoned, to encounter the spirit in its naked state – the spirit that ravens within Ahab's own mind, the secret spirit that works strangely, hidden 'fathom-deep' within the mountainous body of the whale (p. 164). 'If man will strike', he says, 'strike through the mask! How can the prisoner reach outside except by thrusting through the wall?' The white whale, Ahab says, in all its monstrosity, in all its scarcely animate materiality, 'is that wall, shoved near to me', that wall which he must push through in order to encounter the 'inscrutable malice' that animates the whale, the 'unknown reason' that motivates it (p. 145). To encounter the spirit, the 'reasoning thing' that animates the world, we must destroy all matter because, Ahab says, 'truth hath no confines' (p. 145); to discover the whale one would have to strip away the world, to flay the flesh and very bones of things until we are left with Flaubert's unbounded, unconfined nothingness, in which alone one might divine the truth of thought, the thought of truth.

In the figure of Ahab, then, we might see played out on an epic scale the struggle between ideas and things that characterises the positing of the novel body throughout the history of prose fiction. There are very few works in the history of the novel that have captured with this excoriating power the capacity of the creating mind to make its own creations disappear. 'Oh!', cries Ahab. 'How immaterial are all materials! What things real are there but imponderable thoughts' (p. 467). In his obsession with the whale, he takes on the most material of beings, casts himself into the very foundations of the world; but only to demonstrate the ascendency of thought over substance, to reveal to us the non-existence of the material in which thought knows itself. If the task and the duty of the novel is to say a body where there is none, then it is in Ahab's crazed denunciation of his own material being that the novel performs this task and this duty most assiduously. Never has the work of vanishing seemed like a more material effort, or the uncovering of an immateriality that inhabits all materials seemed so hard won. This is creative thinking that leaves a blister on the skin of the mind. This is, in George Eliot's phrase, the most 'arduous' of 'inventions'.[27] But if Ahab's insane artistry is the struggle of ideas to rid themselves of things – some kind of fight to the death between mind and matter – then Melville's own artistry moves in the opposite direction, seeking some kind of accord between them. Where Ahab seeks to overcome the material with the immaterial, Melville's novel seeks a means of understanding their connection, of understanding their mutual dependence upon one another. Ahab might give an expression to the secret non-existence of things, might suggest, with Bowen, that things are made of their indistinctness, their immateriality. Without this non-existence, we would not have the novel, we would not have fiction, or literature, or art. The novel urge is the movement of the non-existent within existent things. But in giving vent to this urge in the demoniacal ravings of Ahab, the mad novelist, Melville seeks to understand how non-existence is seamed into existence, how bodies are made at once of the material and the immaterial, and how the understanding of this compound is the basis for all aesthetics, all politics, all ethics. And, as so often in *Moby Dick*, it is the whale that offers the supreme figure for this bringing together of the idea and the thing, the material and the immaterial. Ahab's hatred for the whale is inspired in part by his desire to scrape away all that excess stuff in which it is clothed. The massiveness of the whale, its material power, offends and injures Ahab, and so he yearns to strip it away, to gain access to that little quivering strand of consciousness which is buried somewhere behind the blank wall of its forehead. But the love that courses through the book, the love of the whale that is balanced against Ahab's hatred, finds extraordinary beauty in this binding of the fugitive will into the sinewy body, in the strange, secret way in which the unimaginable mind of the whale permeates his abundant flesh. Musing on the wonder of the whale's warm blood, its capacity to keep itself warm in icy seas by wrapping around itself a thick coat of its own being, Ishmael suggests that we should take from this a lesson about how we inhabit ourselves, about how our minds might find a dwelling place in our bodies, and in the world. 'Oh man!', Ishmael says, 'admire and model thyself after the whale! Do thou, too, remain warm among ice. Do thou, too, live in this world without being of it' (p. 277).

It is this capacity, to live in the world without being of it, that is the particular gift of the novel to our generation, now, as we seek to reconceive our relations to our transformed bodies and to our sickening planet. It is perhaps the case that one's relation to the world is always composed of this amalgam of belonging and alienation. Consciousness itself is simultaneously the discovery of oneself as a being already present in the world and the intuition of oneself as an idea yet unformed, as an impulse towards being that is always only partly realised in the bodies that we are, or in the hand with which we extend ourselves into the world. But the experience of this partial belonging to the world takes on a particular intensity at times, such as our own, of great transformation. As we enter into the bend of Connor's 'thingly turn' – as the virtualisation of capital and the enormity of eco-catastrophe combine to estrange us from our physical environments, to make things both more thingly and more difficult to animate with ideas – it becomes urgent to rethink the nature of the bonds that hold us in the world. Our understanding of the relation between discursive forms and material embodiment is now in a state of crisis. There is a deep, pervading uncertainty about how information is encoded in being, how ideas relate to things, art to matter, how the tendency of modernity towards virtualisation and electronic disappearance relates to the destruction of our material and ecological environments. The illusion that gripped the west in the last decades of the twentieth century – the idea that being could take place in language, that existence is really an idea unconfined by matter – this illusion has suddenly expired, leaving us with the realisation that we need to rethink the means by which discursive structures are bound into material bodies. It is as if we have collectively awoken, like Stevenson's Dr Jekyll, into a frighteningly real body that is not ours, or only strangely ours, and we have, now, to craft the narratives that will allow us to inhabit it, or at least to negotiate our partial tenancy of it. If this is a task for the new century – if the challenge facing us is to understand better both our immersion within our ailing world and our partial freedom from its material constraints – then it is the novel that is the art form best able to instruct us on how to undertake it. The novel, across its history, conducts the most precise, the most intimate examination of the movement of mind in matter, of the stirring of possible bodies within the bodies that we simply are. In so doing, it offers a history of our future, a means of orienting us within the contours of a body and a world to come.

4 Making Time Matter

> Time is the only narrative that matters.
>
> Don DeLillo, *The Body Artist*[1]

> Time becomes human time to the extent that it is organised after the manner of a narrative.
>
> Paul Ricoeur, *Time and Narrative*[2]

I began the last chapter with Beckett's skeletal depiction of the novelistic scenario. The novel proposes a fictional body, occupying a fictional space. But if these are the two basic elements of the way in which we imagine being, then it is also surely the case that there is a third element, just as foundational to our narrative understanding and depiction of life. In writing fictions we put bodies in space. But we also necessarily put bodies in time. We imagine a body where there is none, in a place where there is none, in a time where there is none.

This requirement – that a body must exist not only in space but also in time – is the subject of a discussion that opens H.G. Wells' classic exploration of the relationship between time and narrative, *The Time Machine*. The unnamed time traveller in Wells' story assembles his guests at the opening of the narrative in order to show them his latest invention, and he prepares them for the unprecedented demonstration they are about to receive by giving them a short lecture on the relationship between time and space. 'The geometry they taught you at school', the traveller says to his friends, 'is founded on a misconception', a fundamental misunderstanding of the nature of spacetime.[3] A body that has only three dimensions, he says – a 'cube', for example, that has 'only length, breadth and thickness' – 'has no real existence' (p. 7). One of the guests, a mildly idiotic character named Filby, interrupts the time traveller. 'There I object', he says, 'Of course a solid body may exist. All real things-.' But we never learn what Filby understands to be the nature of 'real things', because the traveller interrupts him in turn, to qualify his claim that a three-dimensional cube has no existence. 'Can an *instantaneous* cube exist?', he asks his guests. 'Can a cube that does not last for any time at all, have a real existence?' (p. 8). At this, 'Filby became pensive', and the time traveller expands on his theme:

> Clearly any real body must have extension in four directions: it must have Length, Breadth, Thickness, and – Duration. But through a natural infirmity of the flesh we incline to overlook this fact. There are really four dimensions, three which we call the three planes of Space, and a fourth, Time. There is, however, a tendency to draw an unreal distinction between the former three dimensions and the latter, because it happens that our consciousness moves intermittently in one direction along the latter from the beginning to the end of our lives. (p. 8)

Any given body, Wells' inventor declares, is extended not only in space but in time. Indeed, as the physicist Sir Arthur Eddington puts it in his influential 1920 account of Einstein's general theory of relativity, *Time, Space and Gravity*, a body has a far greater extension in time than it has in space. 'An individual', Eddington writes, 'is a four-dimensional object of greatly elongated form; in ordinary language we say that he has considerable extension in time and insignificant extension in space'.[4] Each individual picture we may have of ourselves, or of any other body, might be thought of, Wells' inventor says, as a three-dimensional snapshot of a much larger being that is spread out over time as well as space. 'For instance', he says,

> here is a portrait of a man at eight years old, another at fifteen, another at seventeen, another at twenty-three, and so on. All these are evidently sections, as it were, Three-Dimensional representations of his Four-Dimensioned being, which is a fixed and unalterable thing. (p. 9)

Any portrait of a body simply occupying space would thus necessarily be a partial one, incomplete almost to the point of mendacity. A body in a space can only exist if it is also stretched across time.

This might seem, as we read the beginning of *The Time Machine*, to be very clear. But the persuasive simplicity of the traveller's explanation of time as a fourth dimension varnishes thinly over a great difficulty that is native to our conception of time – a difficulty that perhaps explains the 'natural infirmity of our flesh' which prevents us from seeing time as simply another kind of space. To suggest that time is another dimension, like length or breadth, is to suggest that time has substance, that it is a kind of material that can be laid out or measured. But the difficulty that faces all those who have tried properly to understand temporality is that time seems not to have any material being, seems not to *exist* in the way that we are accustomed to understanding existence. Saint Augustine gives perhaps the most enduring account of this problem in his *Confessions*, written in AD 397–8. 'What, then, is time?', Augustine famously asks himself in Book XI, admitting that this is a question that may be beyond his philosophical power to answer. 'I know well enough what it is', he says rather winningly, 'provided that nobody asks me; but if I am asked what it is and try to explain, I am baffled.'[5] This bafflement, Augustine goes on to demonstrate, emerges from a peculiar fugitive quality to time, whereby all of the tenses in which we might encounter or account for it seem to melt before our gaze. We think of time, Augustine suggests, in terms of three categories: past time, present time and future time. But each of these kinds of time cannot have any existence. Take, first, the present moment. This is the mode of temporality which should perhaps have the most over-powering presence for us; as Elizabeth Bowen puts it, 'the moment, with its apparent reality, dwarfs and confuses us'.[6] But when one tries to isolate the moment, one finds that it continually evades us, slipping away into the past or the future, presenting itself as that which has just happened, or that which is about to happen. 'In fact', Augustine says, 'the only time that can be called present is an instant', and the instant, to prevent itself from being broken into separate moments of past and future time, has to be of absolutely no duration at all. 'If its duration were prolonged', Augustine says, 'it could be divided into past and future', so the present must have no extension, and so, in turn, as Wells' traveller might have told us, the present, like the instantaneous cube, cannot exist (p. 266). But if this then leads us to imagine that the past is where time might truly be said to exist, or the future, Augustine quickly and effectively demonstrates that both these categories of temporality are equally non-existent. 'If the future and the past do exist', Augustine says, 'I want to know where they are.' Moments in the future, he says, 'do not yet exist'; moments in the past 'no longer exist'. The only kind of time that is existing now is the present, but, as he has already demonstrated, that does not exist either. So how, he asks, do we experience time, how do we measure it? 'My mind,' he says, 'is burning to solve this intricate puzzle'. 'To what period do we relate time when we measure it as passing', he asks:

> To the future, from which it comes? No: because we cannot measure what does not [yet] exist. To the present, through which it is passing? No: because we cannot measure what has no duration. To the past, then, towards which it is going? No again: because we cannot measure what no longer exists. (p. 270)

As Augustine says, we know well enough what time is, as long as nobody asks us to explain it. But when we try to look at it, when we try to focus on it so that it might resolve itself into some kind of measurable substance, we find always that it evaporates, that duration as an experience, however fundamental to being it may be – however impossible it is to imagine living, even for an instant, without it – cannot quite yield itself to explanation. 'We cannot rightly say what time *is*', Augustine concludes rather wearily. When we talk of time, 'our use of words is generally inaccurate and seldom completely correct, but our meaning is recognised none the less' (p. 269). We live in time blindly, without being able to measure it or define it, measuring ourselves collectively only to our collective ignorance of its true quality.

So, when Wells' time traveller imagines time as a solid substance, a fourth dimension, he is addressing in part a difficulty that has perplexed our attempts to understand temporal experience at least since Augustine. *The Time Machine*, more than a science fiction fantasy about time travel, is an attempt, at a critical moment in the history of modernity, to imagine how the experience of time as crisis fits within a longer conception of time as fixed or completed. The end of the nineteenth century sees massive changes to the way that time and space are produced and experienced, as capitalist modernity enters into a new phase in its development – changes which produce the classically fin de siècle experience of temporal rupture. The time itself, in the passage from the nineteenth to the twentieth century, seems to be breaking open, falling into a strange and difficult gap between what C.F.G. Masterman in 1905 calls a 'past still showing faint survivals of vitality' and a 'future but hardly coming to birth'.[7] Wells' time machine itself is a symptom of this transformation. The machine echoes contemporary technologies that are rapidly transforming our conception of time and space, closely resembling at once a motor vehicle and a proto cinematic device. But it also seeks to overcome this experience of rapid change, which has such a terrifying, emptying effect on the moment itself, by enabling the traveller to place this moment of historical transformation into a vast temporal schema that stretches from the beginning to the end of planetary history, and that exists with a kind of fixity that the experience of the present moment lacks. And what is so fascinating about this experiment in imagining time travel is that, throughout, Wells casts the capacity to travel physically through time on his imaginary machine as a corollary to the way that narrative itself makes time present to us. The Time Machine is the name, of course, both of the traveller's invention and of Wells' narrative, and throughout it is clear that Wells is testing the power of narrative to overcome the experience of temporal disappearance that arises specifically from fin de siècle anxiety, and more generally from the kinds of philosophical contradictions rehearsed by Augustine. Wells' tale itself enacts an intricate play with temporality. The story takes up the space of a week in the 'present' of the text – from the traveller's initial demonstration of his time machine to his guests to the dinner party with the same guests that takes place a week later – but within the parameters of this week, the traveller crosses the vastest oceans of time, reaching far beyond the decline of the human and towards the death of the sun. And, in doing so, it demonstrates the capacity of narrative fiction at once to occupy a moment, to narrate a rather extraordinarily mobile present and to place that moving present within a lager completed narrative that does not change, that is a 'fixed and unalterable thing'. The narrative itself offers to solve the problems that it addresses, allowing us at once to experience the moment in the midst of its passing, and to situate such a moving present within a past and a future that maintain their reality, despite the fact that they are not yet, or are no longer.

Indeed, it is possible to imagine that this capacity at once to reproduce the experience of being in the moment and to maintain the shape of a fixed temporal scheme or plot that is not eroded by the very unfolding of the moment, is the great gift that the novel has given to our understanding of time. To shape time in accordance with a larger historical logic is, of course, what the novel is able to do, more consummately than any other art form. As Peter Brooks has argued, the history of the novel from Defoe onwards is the story of the novel's increasing capacity to *plot* – to shape time in such a way that we experience both the process of becoming, the giddyingly exciting sensation of passing through time in suspenseful ignorance of what comes next, and the reassurance of a shape to passing time, which anchors the beginning of the story, and the end, within some fixed dimension.[8] It is perhaps the greatest existential difficulty faced by every sensate being that both the beginning of things and the end seem inconceivable. How can we imagine something starting – our lives, for example? It is tremendously difficult, because of course, in order to imagine the beginning we are led to imagine something before the beginning, a state of nothingness before things began from which things somehow emerged, and this we feel we cannot do. As Saint Augustine asks himself in his deliciously semi-comic way, 'What was God doing before he made heaven and earth?' (p. 262). God is infinite, so before the beginning of creation he must have been hanging around, not for a few hundred or a few thousand years, but for all eternity, drumming his fingers, paring his nails. Why would he do that? Whatever was he waiting for? And equally, death confounds our attempt to conceive of it, because in order to imagine ending, we have to imagine the impossible idea of something that comes after the end. Death, as Hamlet immeasurably famously puts it, is 'a consummation devoutly to be wished';[9] it is only death that completes our lives, consummates us as full beings whose story is complete; but death cannot be experienced, or even properly contemplated, because we can't pass beyond it, to see the boundary it represents, Hamlet's 'bourn' (3.1.81), from the other side. But it is this problem that narrative so beautifully addresses; in fact, narrative solves this problem so consummately, in a way that is so closely interwoven with our own sense-making mechanisms, that it is difficult to imagine living without narrative, difficult to imagine living in that waste of unmarked time that greets Crusoe at the opening of *Robinson Crusoe*. As George Eliot puts it in the first sentence of *Daniel Deronda*, with her characteristically wriggling intelligence, 'Men can do nothing without the make-believe of a beginning' (p. 3). We know that the beginning is inconceivable; we know, as Eliot puts it in that same opening, that 'no retrospect will take us to the true beginning' (p. 3). But the beauty of narrative is that it allows us to experience the impossibility of beginning, the impossibility of ending, again and again, even if we are constantly aware of the fictionality of these beginnings, the fact that they are 'make-believe'. From Tristram Shandy's imagining the moment of his own conception (his mother interrupting his father, at the moment of the patriarchal orgasm, to ask him if he has remembered to wind up the clock!), to Malone's dramatising of the moment of his own death, the novel has passed repeatedly beyond Hamlet's bourn from which no traveller ever returns, to bring back news from the other side, from that nowhere that lies before the beginning and after the end.

It is perhaps this capacity that leads Mark Currie, in his subtle and sophisticated discussion of narrative temporality *About Time*, to suggest that the novel produces a specific kind of temporal knowledge, that the novel allows us to 'know' time in a way that no other mode of thinking can. For Currie, the question of what 'value fictional narrative might hold for a philosophical understanding of time'[10] is bound up with the possibility that fiction can help us to negotiate and experience time in a way that philosophy alone cannot. Because fiction does not simply speculate on the peculiar unthinkability of time, but actually reproduces the simultaneous inescapability of the moment and its disappearance into a non-existent past and future, fictional narrative allows for a particular kind of embedded analysis of the texture of lived temporal experience. 'Fictional narrative', Currie argues, 'and narrative in general, offers a kind of access, perhaps the only access we have, to what might be called the 'reality' of time'

(p. 138). If, as Paul Ricoeur argues in his influential work *Time and Narrative*, 'time becomes human time to the extent that it is organised after the manner of a narrative' (p. 3), then it follows that narrative itself is the privileged mode in which to test this becoming meaningful of time. As Ricoeur puts it much later in *Time and Narrative*, fiction offers a 'powerful means of detecting the infinitely varied way of combining the perspective of time that speculation by itself fails to mediate'.[11] It is not simply that prose narrative helps, as in Crusoe's journal, to make time matter in the sense of making time meaningful, bringing it under the purview of some overarching plot. It is also that it helps to make time matter, in that it allows us to grasp something like a material being of time, even as time itself continually evades philosophical knowledge; and, what is more, it does so without misrecognising time, or forcing it into a system of thinking that it resists, as Augustine arguably squeezes his disappearing time into a theological system in his *Confessions*.

In Marcel Proust's monumental work *Remembrance of Things Past*, for example, time is given a material being, in a way that is true, paradoxically, to the non-existence of time, rather than in any sense a philosophical or critical antidote to it. Proust's novel opens, famously, with an experience of the odd disobedience of time – with the contemplation of a past that seems wholly vivid, but which remains absolutely inaccessible to us, abandoned to the non-existence of lost time. Tormented by the presence of a remembered past that will not leave him, but will not come back to him, Marcel thinks in this opening that the past is 'in reality all dead'.[12] 'It is a labour in vain to attempt to recapture it', he thinks, 'all the efforts of our intellect must prove futile' (p. 47). But the entire philosophical and poetic effort of Proust's novel is to find a means of bringing this strange simultaneous presence and absence of the past – the past as the place in which we live, but also as the place in which we are absolutely, irrecoverably lost – into some new kind of alignment. By the time we reach the end of this massive experiment, when we have made the long journey from the 'Overture' to the final, luminous book entitled 'Time Regained', we find with Marcel, to quote the famous line from Faulkner, that 'the past is never dead, it is not even past'.[13] The close of the novel sees

Marcel discovering what he calls 'this notion of Time embodied, or years past and not separated from us', which, he says, 'it was now my intention to emphasise as strongly as possible in my work'.[14] He discovers, by the end of the novel, something like that fourth dimension that Wells' traveller introduces to his guests at the opening of *The Time Machine*. He develops a means of seeing and feeling, 'unrolled in its vast length, the whole of the past which I was not aware that I carried about me' (p. 1105). At the close of the novel, rather than living in a single moment, closed off the from the endless past which lies beneath it, Marcel finds himself stretched, like the four-dimensional portrait imagined by Wells' inventor, across the unnumbered years, extended within what he calls 'this vast dimension which I had not known myself to possess' (p. 1106). His intention in his work, he thinks in the final line of the novel, is to

> describe men first and foremost as occupying a place, a very considerable place compared with the restricted one which is allotted to them in space, a place on the contrary prolonged past measure – for simultaneously, like giants plunged into the years, they touch epochs that are immensely far apart, separated by the slow accretion of many, many days – in the dimension of Time. (p. 1107)

Just as Arthur Eddington draws our attention from our 'insignificant extension in space' to our 'considerable extension in time', so Marcel discovers a means of seeing what Eddington calls our 'greatly elongated form', our material being in time, stretched out across the years. But what it is crucial to understand about this discovery is that it is made not by *denying* the disappearance, the immateriality of time, but by immersing oneself in the evanescent medium of time itself, by attuning oneself to the peculiar harmonies between narrative and time, by finding *in* the inaccessibility of the past the reality of its uncannily vivid presence. It is the specific quality of prose narrative – the fact that narrative both contains time and allows it to pass or flow away – that enables Marcel to undertake his extraordinary project of temporal recovery.

So, as Currie argues, we might suggest that one of the values of the novel is its capacity to make of time – the archetypal fugitive – something 'fixed and unalterable'; or, as Virginia Woolf's Lily Briscoe famously puts it in *To the Lighthouse*, to 'make of the moment something permanent'.[15] One of the greatest achievements of the novel is that it helps us to know time, and perhaps somehow to master it, just as Wells' time traveller masters time. But if we are to understand the nature of this knowing, if we are to understand the way that fictional narrative makes time matter, we have to grasp also that narrative works in the apparently opposite direction; narrative might master time, might make time knowable to us, but it also and at the same time breaks time open, undoing those bonds that habitually tie us to the official passing of time, making of the passing of time something *unknowable*, *unmastered*. And the key thing to grasp here is that this is not only a contradiction in the narrative depiction of time, it is also the very kind of truth about time, the very kind of knowledge, that narrative helps us to acquire. To know time in the way that the novel knows time is to know something of its unknowability, and to live with that knowledge, to make a home for oneself in it. I argued in the last chapter that the novel body is composed of an amalgam of the existent and the non-existent. To understand the novel body is to understand something of its difference from itself, to attune oneself to what Elizabeth Bowen calls the 'indistinctness' of things. To understand novel time, similarly, is to tune oneself to the ways in which time continually makes bodies different from themselves. If there is an indistinctness at the heart of things, if bodies are only ever semblances of themselves, then this is perhaps partly because time takes us repeatedly away from ourselves. As Samuel Beckett puts it in his short book on Proust, in completing his or her journey through life 'the subject has died – and perhaps many times – on the way'.[16] 'We are not merely more weary because of yesterday', he argues, 'we are other, no longer what we were before the calamity of yesterday' (p. 13). To be in time is constantly to die, constantly to abandon versions of 'our many selves' (p. 31) on the roadside, as if casting off jumpers. And this is part of what the novel knows. It may be that prose fiction helps us to extend ourselves over time, helps us to see a four-dimensional continuity that binds the portrait of ourselves at fifteen to another portrait at seventeen, and another at twenty-three. But it does so only to the extent that it summons this continuity – as we ourselves do in 'life' – from an intimate contact with the discontinuity that intervenes between each moment and the next, that makes the passage from moment to moment, as Don DeLillo puts it, feel like a 'quantum hop'.[17] As Currie argues, the experience of being in time means that 'presence requires a kind of self-distance' (p. 150), that presence itself is divided by the work of time within us; and the fictional narration of time does not protect us from this fact, but emerges from it. This is why, Currie argues, 'fiction cannot operate with a notion of undivided presence as its guiding concept' (p. 150); fiction itself comes into being as it registers the difference from self that is part of every narrative reflection – the distance that it is the job of narrative both to open, and to close.

There is perhaps no single novel that has investigated this disjuncture between measured and unmeasured time more closely, and more influentially, than Virginia Woolf's 1925 novel *Mrs Dalloway*. If the modernist novel collectively – from Proust's masterpiece to Joyce's *Ulysses* to William Faulkner's *The Sound and the Fury* – can be seen as an extended experiment in the narration of a mobile temporality, it is Woolf's novel that comes the closest, I think, to following and reproducing the tumbling, gathering, dispersing movement of being in time. This is a novel that is entranced by the experience of becoming over time, and works with extraordinary inventiveness and formal suppleness to reproduce this experience. Set, famously, on a single day in June 1923, and following closely the passage of this single day from morning, through afternoon to evening, the novel produces a remarkably innovative technique that allows the narrator to reach freely through time, tracing the remembered past of each of the major characters as it gathers beneath the thin surface of the passing day. While the traveller in Wells' *Time Machine* imagines a composite four-dimensional portrait made up of snapshots of a single character at various stages of life, Woolf's novel manages actually to produce this narrative portrait for us, looking on as the characters' minds skip freely from youth to adolescence to middle age, gathering together all of these discrete moments into something like a fullness of being. In one of the central images of the novel, the main character, Clarissa Dalloway, pictures this accumulation of a lived life. As

Clarissa allows her mind to wander back through the memories of her childhood and youth, she is overcome, like Proust's Marcel, by a sense of the presence of her past, by the co-existence of her youth and her late middle age, and she feels an urge to somehow show the life that she has lived to her parents (now dead) for their approval or their blessing. 'For she was a child', she thinks,

> throwing bread to the ducks, between her parents, and at the same time a grown woman coming to her parents who stood by the lake, holding her life in her arms which, as she neared them, grew larger and larger in her arms, until it became a whole life, a complete life, which she put down by them and said, 'This is what I have made of it! This!'[18]

Throughout the novel, this image of accumulation, of the gathering together of being, grows in weight, just as Clarissa imagines her life gaining weight in her arms. As the narrative moves across time and between the characters that make up the story, it gathers together not only Clarissa's memories, but those of the other characters, producing a kind of mingling of present and past, one person and another, allowing for an intense experience of shared recall in which one feels oneself spread out, like Marcel's giants plunged in the years, across a recovered temporal dimension.

But if *Mrs Dalloway* seeks to give expression to a version of Wells' fourth dimension, if it is fascinated by the experience of becoming over time, it nevertheless offers, at the same time, an extraordinarily impassioned refusal of the principle of temporal accumulation. While seeking to gather moments together into a kind of bundle, to preserve time, to make of it 'something permanent', the novel develops one of the sharpest critiques we have of the means by which we measure and archive the passage through time, the means by which we think of ourselves as beings extended across the days and the years. The gathering together of time in *Mrs Dalloway* is a matter of personal becoming, but it is also the effect of a repressive imperial politics – official time as the unfolding of a patriarchal order. The passage of the narrative through the course of the day is punctuated by the striking of the imposingly phallic Big Ben – 'first a warning, musical; then the hour, irrevocable' (p. 2) – and the central concern of the narrative is to watch as this authoritative marking of time gives a shape to all of the various timelines that the novel assembles. The reprise of the novel is that the 'leaden circles dissolve in the air', the sound of the striking of Big Ben spreading like shockwaves, like the ripples from a flung stone, across the space of the city; and, as these shockwaves spread, the novel watches as the force of measured time positions each of the characters within the stories of their own lives. It is not just that the declamatory power of Big Ben forces each of the characters into a homogenous stream of time – the time 'ratified by Greenwich' (p. 114), and sponsored by Rigby and Lowndes ('a commercial clock', the narrator says, 'suspended above a shop in Oxford Street, announced, genially and fraternally, as it if it were a pleasure to Messrs. Rigby and Lowndes to give the information gratis, that it was half past one' (p. 114)). It is not just that this official time shapes and moulds our experience of temporal being, reaching deeply into our time sense and ordering it according to the narrative of nation and of empire; it is that this assertion of the time controls our relation with our own bodies, and with the bodies of others. If the desire of the text is to move freely in time and space – to pass not only from moment to moment but from person to person, as Clarissa and her old friend Peter Walsh pass 'in and out of each other's minds without any effort' (p. 69) – then the striking of Big Ben returns us to ordered time, and to separate subjecthood, to the protocols of sanity, of normality, of self-identity, of proportion. Repeatedly throughout the novel, Clarissa catches sight of an old lady who lives across the street, and this glance, shared between people remote from one another, carries some of the longing in this novel for a kind of telepathic communion, a coming together of mind and mind. But the striking of Big Ben, marking the half hour, imposes, Clarissa thinks, a kind of barrier between them. 'How extraordinary it was', Clarissa thinks as Big Ben strikes, 'to see the old lady move away from the window, as if she were attached to that sound, that string. Gigantic as it was, it had something to do with her. Down, down, into the midst of ordinary things the finger fell' (p. 142). Just as, earlier in the novel, the striking of Big Ben seems to break the connection that Clarissa makes with Peter Walsh ('The sound of Big Ben striking the half-hour struck out between them', the narrator says, 'with extraordinary vigour (p. 52)), so here the leaden announcing of the time forces Clarissa and the old lady to resume their allotted positions in time and space, to conform to the version of themselves decreed by the official account of passing time.

So, when Clarissa imagines her life accumulating in her arms, when she imagines herself becoming over time, her rich sense of accumulation is bound up deeply, irrevocably, with the passage of time as decreed by Big Ben, the authority which shapes us in time, as it imprisons us in our own bodies, within our individual narrative units. And, as entranced as the novel is with the emergence of self over time, its political and aesthetic energies are ranked against this regulated becoming, this forced adoption of a prescribed character in an unfolding narrative. For both Clarissa and the other central character of the novel – the traumatised war veteran Septimus Warren Smith – the meting out of official time by Big Ben is experienced as a kind of assault, which for Clarissa is the 'forcing of the soul' (p. 208) and for Septimus is the brutal 'overriding of opposition', whereby time itself 'stamp[s] indelibly in the sanctuaries of others the image of herself' (p. 114). The clock, in measuring time, in 'shredding and slicing, dividing and subdividing' the 'mound of time' in which we live, works, the narrator says, to 'uphold authority', to instil a 'sense of proportion', to navigate us into our allotted roles. And for both Clarissa and Septimus, the political and aesthetic response to this enforced proportion is to seek to escape from measured time, to improvise an exit from that four-dimensional being that Wells' traveller speaks of at the beginning of *The Time Machine*, that material duration that makes of time a 'fixed and unalterable thing'. For Septimus, this escape takes the form of suicide, the realisation of the potential death that lies in wait within the seams of all measured time. If the measured accumulation of time is the force that corrals us into regulated being, if this is what instils in us the sense of proportion prescribed by the authoritarian doctors who 'treat' Septimus' post-traumatic shock, then Septimus chooses death as the refusal of time. For Clarissa, such refusal takes perhaps the opposite form. Where Septimus chooses death, Clarissa chooses what she calls 'life'; this is what she 'loved', she thinks to herself, 'life; London; this moment in June' (p. 2). To immerse oneself in life, she thinks, is to give oneself up entirely to the present, to the passing moment, where one is most truly alive. It is to abandon any notion of accumulation over time, to abandon that fully grown life that she holds in her arms and presents to her parents. One shouldn't remember, she thinks; 'everyone remembered; what she loved was this, here, now, in front of her' (p. 7). To live is to be 'plunged into the very heart of the moment', the 'moment of this June morning on which was the pressure of all the other mornings' (p. 39). To live in time is not to accumulate moment upon moment, but to separate the moment off, to 'transfix' it (p. 39), to lift it from the temporal flow. Yet if this seems like the opposite of Septimus' suicide, like the immersion in the living moment rather than the suicidal ejection from it, what this novel discovers is that these two forms of refusal are in some ways the same. 'She felt somehow very like him' (p. 210), Clarissa says, as she learns of Septimus' death; and indeed, the experience of immersion in the stilled moment is a kind of intense living that is also a willed death. The moment only becomes meaningful, only *matters*, when it is placed within a narrative plot, when it becomes an extension of the past, or a foretaste of the future. When it stands on its own, as in times of great happiness or great grief, its plenitude is also an emptiness, its trembling living is a stilled death. As Clarissa thinks to herself when she experiences the kind of pleasure that stops the moment, that leaves her becalmed in stationary time, to experience time this intensely is to undergo a kind of death. 'If it were now to die', she thinks to herself, with Shakespeare's Othello, ''twere now to be most happy' (p. 37; 2.1.190–1).

Mrs Dalloway, then, rehearses a kind of contradiction between the capacity of narrative to assemble time, to organise it in terms of a plot, and its opposite capacity to catch at the resistance of passing time to the demands of such a plot. And in doing so, it demonstrates, as Mark Currie puts it, that fictional narrative is able to know time more fully, more intimately, than any other kind of speculation. If, as Augustine suggests, time both consists in its division into past, present and future, and escapes the expressive power of each of these tenses, then it is fictional narrative that captures this contradiction in both of its modes, that captures time as accumulation and time as the radically non-accumulable. One of the great achievements of *Mrs Dalloway* is its capacity to express this temporal contradiction both aesthetically and politically. The novel offers an extraordinarily sharp articulation of the ways in which political power – the ideological regimes that determine the narrative quality of time and of history – is implicated in the most intimate experience of passing time. To extend oneself in time is to become part of a plot, to accept a temporal logic and a sense of 'proportion' that is to some extent alien to us, to some extent an ideological imposition. But to refuse such a plot is to confine oneself to the precincts of a moment that, for all its intensity, can only come to us as a kind of death. It is in the moment, perhaps, in the instant that has no duration, that we are most fully and freely ourselves; but, of course, it is in the moment that we have no self at all, none of the attributes of memory or anticipation that make us into ourselves. To know time is to know this terrible vibration between historical extension and instantaneous being, this terrible demand that one becomes oneself only by continually losing oneself. *Mrs Dalloway* seems to present us with a choice between two forms of dying, as the only means of escape from the authorities who would force our soul, who would stamp, in our innermost sanctuaries, images of themselves. We die by abandoning the moment, by leaping from windows onto the palings below; or we die by plunging into the moment, by drowning in the still waters of arrested time. Either way, to know time is to know that becoming is necessarily a kind of loss, redeemable only by the consummation of a chosen death.

But if this is the kind of knowledge of time that fiction appears to afford us – a rather gloomy kind of knowledge, perhaps! – then it is crucial also to understand that prose narrative generates, itself, a kind of time of its own. The value of the novel might lie in part in its capacity to critique the regimes that determine the passing of time, and in its ability to help us know the contradictions that living in time produces. But it is also the case that the novel has a particular capacity to craft new time signatures, new temporal forms which enable or even require us to think the time differently. In *Mrs Dalloway*, this new temporality takes the form of what Judith

Halberstam and others have called a kind of 'queer time'.[19] There is an implicit connection, throughout *Mrs Dalloway*, between the measured passing of time – with the 'sense of proportion' that such measure assumes – and what we might call a compulsory heterosexuality. The force that drives us through the day from past to future is also the force that presses both Clarissa and Septimus towards conventionality, towards the adoption of a set of normative behaviours. This is the force that leads Septimus' employer to urge him, as an antidote to his intellectual sensitivity and his effeminacy, to take up football (p. 95), and that leads Clarissa herself to marry Richard Dalloway, to become 'not even Clarissa any more', but 'Mrs. Richard Dalloway' (p. 9). But against this pressure towards the heteronormative, the novel offers a series of alternative shapes, formal patterns which gesture towards another mode of becoming. These alternatives are organised around homoerotic desire – Clarissa's desire for Sally Seton, Septimus' desire for Evans – but they also emerge from a kind of revolutionary textual principle, a poetic means of putting together narrative time that does not obey the dictats of Big Ben, or of Rigby and Lowndes. As the novel charts and is itself shaped by the linear passage of the day, from morning to night, it also produces an extraordinary poetic undertow, the possibility of another temporal logic, which gathers under the surface of the text and which suggests not only a different way of thinking about the relation between past and present, but also between one person and another. This undertow, a kind of submerged homoerotic undercurrent, is generated not at the level of plot, not by the engine which pushes the narrative forward, but at the level of form and through a delicate series of assonant associations that gather around the experience of transgressive desire. Take, for example, Clarissa's reflections on her desire for Sally, on her tendency, when yielding to the 'charm of a woman', to 'feel what men felt':

> Only for a moment; but it was enough. It was a sudden revelation, a tinge like a blush which one tried to check and then, as it spread, one yielded to its expansion, and rushed to the furthest verge and there quivered and felt the world come closer, swollen with some astonishing significance, some pressure of rapture, which split its thin skin and gushed and poured with extraordinary alleviation over the cracks and sores! Then, for that moment,

she had seen an illumination; a match burning in a crocus; an inner meaning almost expressed. But the close withdrew; the hard softened. It was over – the moment. (p. 34)

This evocation of orgasm in some ways follows the heteronormative logic of the novel. The swelling and dwindling motion captured here – the tendency for the moment to light up with erotic fire before dying out, for the hard to soften, the close to withdraw – suggests that moments of intensity are contained within an onward passage of time which continually empties them of their power. But what is most striking about this passage is that it returns again and again in the novel, in its sounds and its central images, and in doing so it produces a kind of fragile centre to the novel, an enclave made only of rhyme and rhythm, where another kind of time, another kind of intersubjectivity, might subsist. The image of a breaking skin, which allows an inside to leak out, for example, catches echoes and shards from moments across the novel. It appears, slightly morphed, in the recurring image of the breaking wave, Woolf's preferred sign, in *Mrs Dalloway*, *The Waves* and *To the Lighthouse*, for the liquid passage of time. Thinking of plunging into the sea, as an analogue to plunging into the moment, Clarissa imagines diving into 'the waves which threaten to break, but only gently split their surface, roll and conceal and encrust as they just turn over the weeds with pearl' (p. 32). And then, later, Septimus picks up and harmonises with these associations between time, orgasm and the splitting of the skin. His wife Rezia asks him what time it is, and the question opens for him, in his madness, onto an 'astonishing revelation' (p. 78) that echoes Clarissa's 'sudden revelation', her discovering of 'astonishing significance', and that mingles with Septimus' memories of Evans and the violence of time in taking him away. 'The word "time" split its husk', Septimus thinks, and 'poured its riches over him' (p. 77), just as the lifting wave splits its thin skin, just as 'the pressure of rapture' splits the skin in the midst of Clarissa's imagined orgasm. And then, at the climax of the novel, as Clarissa learns of Septimus' suicide, all of these associations come back in a rush, where they evoke Clarissa's love for Sally, Septimus' love for Evans, and the desire that thrills through the text for a kind of becoming that does not involve the adoption of a prescribed role, a kind of becoming that might allow for an intimate, unbroken encounter with the other, a rapturous pouring out of the skin of the self. 'A thing there was that mattered', Clarissa thinks, as she reflects on Septimus' suicide:

> a thing wreathed about with chatter, defaced, obscured in her own life, let drop every day in corruption, lies, chatter. This he had preserved. Death was defiance. Death was an attempt to communicate, people feeling the impossibility of reaching the centre which, mystically, evaded them; closeness drew apart; rapture faded; one was alone. There was an embrace in death. (p. 208)

This is an extraordinary moment in the novel, a moment of intense sympathy, when the two central characters, occupying separate halves of the narrative, enter into a kind of union, one that is not ratified by the official temporal and spatial protocols of the plot, but which takes place in those underground spaces that the novel fashions out of the rhythms of the prose. Hearing of Septimus' death, Clarissa recovers those feelings of orgasmic intensity, of revelation and rapture, that she associates with homoerotic desire; this is the inner meaning almost expressed, the centre almost reached. Here, as earlier in the novel, the experience of orgasm, of something intensely shared, yields to the passage of time; closeness draws apart and rapture fades as, earlier, the hard had softened, the close withdrew. But what has happened, by this stage in the novel, is that these terms, these words and rhythms, have produced a kind of network, a kind of tracery which means that passing time is balanced against another kind of time that does not pass, or that passes in a different way. Under this other time signature, the queer time that the novel amasses under its own thin skin, death is not simply the refusal of time, not simply the means by which we are either ejected from the moment or sunk hopelessly within it. Instead, and magically, it has become 'defiance', an 'attempt to communicate'. The death that marks the disappearance of the moment, the failure to live fully and freely in time, has become, here, the means of another kind of temporal consciousness, another kind of experience both of the self, and of the other. Even as the novel's diurnal course takes us from dawn to dusk, from a shared life to a final solitude, this internal tracery works in in the opposite direction, insistently suggesting a means of gathering time, of making it a 'thing that mattered', fashioning a different kind of medium or dimension in which we are able to extend ourselves past our own skins and into the sanctuaries of others.

This, then, is the double gift of the novel to our understanding of time. It both offers a critical analysis of the processes which shape our being in time, and allows us to conceive new kinds of temporality, to imagine a different kind of relationship to passing time than that which is produced by our existing tenses and our existing devices for chronological measurement. This temporal sense is one of the reasons why the novel has been so central to our collective imagination as it has emerged over the course of modernity. And if it has always been the special talent of the novel to fashion a means of 'reckoning time' at key moments in the history of modernity – as Crusoe stands on his desolate beach, as Wells' time traveller mounts his cinematic machine, as Joyce and Woolf seek to produce a time machine that can negotiate the modernist city, as the great novelists of decolonisation seek to produce a time signature of the postcolony – then our own historical period is perhaps itself a transformative moment, a moment in which modernity is entering a new phase. Where modernism was shaped by the advent of twentieth-century modernity – the arrival of steam travel and cinema as technologies that transformed the relationship between space and time – our time is bent and reshaped by the unfolding of an information revolution that is potentially as transformative as the industrial revolution of the eighteenth and nineteenth centuries. And alongside this rapid evolution in the technological production of time, we are living in the midst of a new apocalypticism that is utterly transforming our sense of planetary time. Where the previous generation lived with the time sense produced by the imminence of nuclear destruction, we are living with the ticking of a different kind of clock. During the writing of this book, the IPCC environmental agency issued a report which confirmed that some of our 'ecosystems are already experiencing irreversible regime shifts' – that is, that some of the damage done to the environment by human pollution is irreversible.[20] The history of human industrial 'progress' has brought us to the point where we have already permanently destroyed parts of our environment, which means that we are living in an apocalypse that has already arrived, that is truly 'now'.

Under these conditions, the novel today is faced with a difficult task. How to tell the time, when the widest of gulfs have opened up between a 'human time' that is moving too strangely, too fast and too slow to be recorded by any clock, and a planetary time that is now asserting its own implacable and anti-human logic. As Don DeLillo puts it, in his late masterpiece *The Body Artist*, it seems that we have lost our bearings in this newly passing, postmillennial time. We seem, as DeLillo's narrator says, no longer to 'know how to measure [ourselves] to what we call the now' (p. 66). In an echo of Augustine, whose *Confessions* haunts DeLillo's novel, the narrator recognises that the 'now' has always been elusive. What is the now anyway, he asks. 'It's possible there's no such thing, for those who do not take it as a matter of faith' (pp. 66–67). Time, he says, sharing Augustine's beautiful bafflement, 'is the thing you know nothing about' (p. 98). But if narrative has always had to sculpt an elusive now into a kind of consecutive order, DeLillo's novel is responding to a scenario in which narrative itself has lost its grip on time. The novel initiates us into a 'kind of reality' in which we are 'here and there, before and after', in which we move 'from one to the other shatteringly, in a state of collapse' (p. 64), and into a 'kind of time that ha[s] no narrative quality' (p. 65).

Ricoeur's response to the elusiveness of time, as we have seen, is to assert a mutually productive relationship between narrative and the human. 'Time becomes human time', he says, 'to the extent that it is organized after the manner of a narrative' (p 1). But our time, perhaps, requires us to respond to the possibility that narrative can no longer tune itself to the human, that narrative needs to find another organising principle. The narrator of the *Body Artist* declares, in what seems almost to be a tautology, that 'time is the only narrative that matters'. 'Time is what makes us', the protagonist Lauren thinks to herself. 'You are made out of time', she says. 'This is the force that tells you who you are. Close your eyes and feel it. It is time that defines your existence' (p. 92). But if it is time that 'matters', time that makes meaning, and that makes matter, then *The Body Artist* explores the possibility that this force is not a human force, but one which we have to encounter outside the realms of the human. As Richard Powers puts it, in his extraordinary story of ecological catastrophe *The Seventh Event*, to think the time now, in the midst of what we still call 'climate change', we have to think beyond the 'gauge of the human'.[21] There is a powerful movement in world literature today that seeks to do just that, that seeks to break the relationship between narrative and the human, to allow us to see time differently, to retune our relationship not only with the time of our transformed culture, but with the time of the planet. In *The Body Artist*, this approach to nonhuman time is conducted through the shared gaze of the animal. Just as Clarissa is entranced by the caught glance of the old lady opposite her, *The Body Artist* – a novel engaged in a rich dialogue with Woolf – turns around the gaze that Lauren shares with a bird who perches outside her kitchen window. 'When birds look into houses', Lauren thinks, 'what impossible worlds they see.' 'Think', she goes on, 'what shedding of every knowable surface and process' (p. 22). The bird, in stripping surface, in eluding process, sees, Lauren thinks, 'the apparition of a space set off from time' (p. 22) and it is just this apparition, this capacity to see without the processes and surfaces of human time, that the novel calls for now. As Lauren looks at the bird through her kitchen window, as she seeks to feel the time that makes her, to feel the 'flow of time in her body, to tell her who she was' (p. 124), she is drawing on the resources of the novel to see time differently, to craft new ways of metabolising the passing of time. *The Body Artist*, in its dialogue with Woolf, in its dialogue with the longer history of fiction, knows that the novel has always been able to carry within itself a time that cannot quite come to tense or to knowledge – a time that has no narrative quality. Lauren's glance at the bird contains Clarissa's glance at the old woman, as it contains the endlessly strange glance that Ishmael shares with the whale in *Moby Dick*. 'Time began with man', Ishmael thinks to himself in a Ricoeurish way; but the consciousness of the whale seems to him to stretch much further, to extend in a dimension that knows nothing of human time. Ishmael is entranced, confounded by the contemplation of this animal time, the time of the 'unsourced existence' of the whale, which, 'having been before all time, must needs exist after all human ages are over' (p. 408). When Lauren looks into the eye of the bird, it is this kind of extended time that she feels, the time that the novel can somehow foreknow, even if it cannot quite capture it in narrative.

It is this time that is the time of the novel – and the time that the novel now has to help us to bring freshly into being, so that we might move towards an unknown future. If the novel has a task now, then it is perhaps more than anything else this – the requirement that we tune ourselves to a new future, that we craft a new shape in which we might encounter the time to come.

5 The Novel, Justice and the Law

> While ignorance and poverty persist on earth, books such as this cannot fail to be of value.
>
> Victor Hugo, *Les Misérables*[1]

> In the final analysis literature, by its very activity, denies the substance of what it represents. That is its law and its truth.
>
> Maurice Blanchot, *The Work of Fire*[2]

> This law is, of course, at present unknown to us.
>
> Fyodor Dostoyevsky, *Crime and Punishment*[3]

If the novel places imaginary bodies in imaginary space and imaginary time, then it also offers imaginary depictions of the laws that operate upon such bodies, the rules by which bodies share space and time with each other. It is perhaps the central, driving desire of the novel to picture worlds which operate according to established rules, in order to gain some understanding of the principles that govern such rules. As Ian McEwan has recently put it, fiction and the law are 'rooted in the same ground';[4] both seek to give accounts of the complicated, diverse ways in which people seek to co-exist, and both apply abstract notions of 'justice' to such interactions. From the appearance of Thomas More's *Utopia* in 1516 – a work which can be considered a prototype of the novel form that developed more fully in the early eighteenth century – the practice of writing fiction has emerged in tandem with the attempt to offer pictures of better worlds, fairer laws, and forms of good governance. Across the centuries of the modern novel's development – from the enlightenment classics of Swift, Voltaire and Wollstonecraft, to the great nineteenth-century works of crime and punishment by Dostoyevsky, Victor Hugo, Charles Dickens and Alexandre Dumas, to the crime and detective novels of Conan Doyle, Edgar Allen Poe and Agatha Christie, to twentieth-century explorations of crime and justice from Thomas Pynchon to Jonathan Littell to Roberto Bolaño – fiction has developed an intricate relationship with legal processes.

Now, one way to think about this relationship between fiction and the law, in the context of a consideration of the value of the novel, is to propose that fiction itself works to shape legal thinking, that it has a kind of responsibility to bring a better, more just world into being. This, indeed, is one of the goals of the utopian thought that sprung up with More's sixteenth-century treatise, and that has been intimately entangled with the passage of the novel from Defoe to Swift to Mary Shelley to H.G. Wells to Charlotte Perkins Gilman to Yevgeny Zamyatin to Margaret Atwood. Utopian fiction, one might argue, offers pictures of perfected worlds which, whilst they are make-believe, non-existent, nevertheless allow us to take a real leap into a better future. The name 'Utopia' itself suggests some such function to utopian imagining. The Greek term *utopia*, like many of the proper nouns in More's deliciously sly text, is an ingenious pun that combines the Greek *eu-topia*, meaning 'good place', with the Greek *ou-topia*, meaning 'no place'. It may be that this pun suggests a certain cynicism on More's part – insinuating, in the very name of his perfect state, that a good place necessarily does not exist – but what More is investigating in *Utopia* is the possibility that fiction, the reporting of non-existent things, is a privileged means of conceiving the good. The non-existent (*ou*), fiction's gift to thought, is fused with the good (*eu*) to produce a picture of the world in which the justice that is yet to come into being in reality is prematurely realised as fiction. Ethical thinking itself involves the struggle to conceive a relationship between the world as it *is* and the world as it *ought to be*. As such, it always involves us in a kind of fiction-making, requiring us to reach into the darkness of a world that is not yet here, whose rules we do not yet understand, in order to imagine how we might change the world that we can see. The ethical imperative requires us continually to reach for a conception of justice that we cannot quite formulate, but which everywhere makes its presence known by our very failure to conceive it. All we really know about the rules by which we live, the laws that govern us, is that they are not just in an absolute sense. They do not fully capture the spirit of the good, the true, because this spirit is not thinkable for us. We do not know what principle governs life in the world so we cannot be properly true to it, we cannot fully codify it, or live by it. The striving for goodness is thus one that takes us continually beyond ourselves, continually into a realm that we can only encounter in its non-existence, in its darkness – that is, as a fiction. The utopian imagination, in blending the non-existent with the good, thus sets out to resolve the tension between 'is' and 'ought', cancelling the difference between the way things are and the way they should be. Every close reader of More's text knows that the perfect island of Utopia is really just an idealised picture of sixteenth-century England, that the traveller to Utopia, Raphael Hythloday, is really a portrait of Thomas More himself, as he (partly) wishes to be. By inventing a startling new fictional form that seamlessly blends the real with the imaginary – the form, of course, that was to become the modern novel – More is able to give a picture of England as it is, which is fused with a picture of its utopian mirror image, an image of England as it ought to be, in which all of the obstacles to the formation of a just state are removed.

Throughout the history of the novel, from More to the present day, one can see this kind of wish fulfilment being played out. The utopian novel, as a genre, offers us pictures of states in which all contradictions have been resolved, which then serve not only to help us to imagine solutions to real problems, but also to understand better what the problems themselves are. More's island is built to counteract a specific set of injustices arising from monarchical power and corruption in early modern Europe; and, in his wake, utopian novels have arisen that address every conceivable form of social problem, by offering a fictional reconciliation of real contradictions. Both utopian fiction and its close relation, the detective novel, seek to conceive of justice by producing scenarios in which existing contradictions have been worked through and resolved. Charlotte Perkins Gilman's 1915 novel *Herland*, for example, offers us a picture of a state in which the imbalance of power between men and women is overcome by the simple expedient of removing sexual difference itself. The novel imagines a land where there are no men (the Herland of the title), and discovers in the process how intrinsic to all forms of public life gender inequality is. With no sexual difference, she discovers, there is no need for conventional notions of individuality, no need for a distinction between public and private, no contradiction between secret longing and the desire for the public good. The absence of men means there are 'no shady places',[5] no hidden elements in the culture which might threaten us, and thus no more historical dynamics left to play out. In the light, ordered, public spaces of Herland, all has been brought out of hiding, all has been revealed, and nothing is left to desire, to strive or long for. Similarly, the crime novel plays out a fantastical overcoming of the obstacles to justice, an eradication of the 'shady places' in which crime might hide, into which justice cannot penetrate. The standard detective formula (subject, of course, to many local variations) allows us to recognise and then resolve criminal tendencies in rather the same way that the horror formula allows us to recognise and overcome the grotesque or the monstrous. In perhaps his most famous utterance, Arthur Conan Doyle's Sherlock Holmes makes of this process a kind of credo. 'How often have I said to you', Holmes says to his slow-witted side-kick Watson in *The Sign of Four*, 'that when you have eliminated the impossible, whatever remains, *however improbable, must be the truth*'.[6] The novel, seen in this light, is an engine for the production of truth, through the elimination of the impossible, the eradication of 'shady places'. As the utopian novel converts the 'not' into the 'good', refashioning the non-existence of fiction as the foundation of ethical thought, so the detective novel converts the falsehood of crime into the truth of detection, by 'eliminating' the impossible, the unknown.

The novel's principle utopian function might be to make justice thinkable in this way – to offer fictional solutions to real problems. But, if this is one way to think about the ethical capacity of the fictional imagination, it is also the case that the ethical charge of the novel works in the other direction – not towards the revelation of ethical truth, or the 'elimination' of the unknown, but rather towards the expression of the unknowable itself as a form of ethical thinking. It may be that one of the values of the novel is its capacity to summon pictures of justice that act as prompts or goads towards better worlds, but this capacity is always troubled by the fact that such pictures of the way things ought to be are necessarily contaminated by the way things are, drawn from the stock of existing things. It is the first objection to utopian thinking, everywhere it is found, that one person's utopia is another person's hell. The novel is perhaps no more immune to bias and partiality than any other form of representation, and in offering pictures of how things should be, it simply offers an account of how a particular author supposes things should be, a picture filtered through the author's own blindnesses and ideological limits (More's 'perfect state', for example, affords no equality for women, and punishes adultery by death). Indeed, for this reason, it might be argued that the novel itself is not a fit vehicle for the espousal of 'values' at all – that a novel which seeks to offer a particular picture of the true or the good suffers a kind of demotion from literature to propaganda. Maurice Blanchot makes this kind of argument when he writes in his 1949 book, *The Work of Fire*, that it is 'futile' for the writer 'to claim to have stable values' or to commit him or herself to 'the seriousness of an ideal' (p. 309). When a novel charges itself with the task of upholding 'values', when it seeks to 'attach itself permanently to a truth outside itself', Blanchot argues, 'it ceases to be literature and the writer who still claims that he is a writer enters into another aspect of bad faith' (p. 310). It is not simply that the values that any novelist endorses are necessarily subjective, propagandistic; it is for Blanchot the case that the task of literature, its very vocation, is to evacuate 'value' as a concept. Literature does not seek to establish the truth of things or to eliminate the uncertain, the impossible; rather, it gives expression to unknowing as kind of condition. 'Literature', he writes, 'by its very activity, denies the substance of what it represents. This is its law and its truth' (p. 310). If utopian thinking tends to convert the 'not' into the 'good', putting the non-existent to work in the service of truth, then Blanchot suggests that 'literature' should move in the opposite direction, continually revealing its own immateriality, taking the insubstantiality of fictional things as its only concern. The only truth that the novel can reveal is the truth of its own non-existence; only in so doing does it rise to the status of 'literature'.

It might be the case, then, that the novel's ethical impulse moves in two directions, both of which tend to undermine its capacity to imagine justice. Either the novel proposes pictures of better worlds, in which case it sacrifices its own aesthetic disinterestedness for a political 'message', becoming a simple didactic machine for the transmission of a 'world view'; or it remains true to its own 'insubstantiality' – to the non-existence that is its law and its truth – in which case it condemns itself to a kind of silence, a kind of absolute distance from the world in which the striving for justice takes place. The novel is caught between propaganda on one hand – Blanchot's 'bad faith' – and the 'rejection of reality' on the other – what Georg Lukács calls an 'escape into nothingness'.[7] But if this problem has disabled the novel's ethical function – encouraging us to erect a false distinction between 'committed' art, which quickly degrades to propaganda, and 'autonomous' art, which appears as a kind of decadent apoliticism – it is also the case, I think, that this working contradiction between substance and the insubstantial, between the material and the immaterial, is where the ethical value of the novel lies.

It is perhaps in the great nineteenth-century explorations of crime and justice, by Hugo, Dostoyevsy, Dumas and others, that this contradiction is worked out most fully. Hugo's masterpiece *Les Misérables*, for example, is driven, at its core, by an investment in the utopian capacity of the novel to bring a revolutionary future into being, to make justice somehow conceivable in fictional form. The story of the ex-convict and recidivist Jean Valjean's attempt to evade the law (manifest in the figure of Javert, the ruthless inspector who hunts Valjean down), and his enmeshment in the sprawling machinery of revolutionary France, is offered by Hugo explicitly as a moral corrective. While the world that we live in is unjust, Hugo writes in the epigraph to the novel, while 'civilisation' is a 'human hell', and 'ignorance and poverty persist on the earth', then 'books such as this cannot fail to be of value' (p. 15). It is the task of *Les Misérables* to narrate to us the moral awakening of Jean Valjean, and the revolutionary awakening of France, and in doing so to trace what the narrator calls a 'convulsive movement towards the ideal' (p. 1048), to 'lift the veil' that covers the idea of social progress, or 'at least let a clear light shine through it' (p. 1048). 'The book which the reader now holds in his hands', the narrator says,

> from one end to the other, as a whole and in its details, treats of the advance from evil to good, from injustice to justice, from falsity to truth, from darkness to daylight, from blind appetite to conscience, from decay to life, from bestiality to duty, from Hell to Heaven, from limbo to God. (pp. 1048–9)

Hugo's novel, like Dostoyevsky's *Crime and Punishment*, is entirely focused on divining and then tracing the possibility of justice as it makes itself felt within the injustice of contemporary reality. Both novels are gripped by the conviction, as Dostoyevsky's Sonya puts it, that 'there must be justice in everything'.[8] Both stake everything on Raskolnikov's belief, in *Crime and Punishment*, that 'the order that governs the way in which people come into the world . . . must be very accurately and precisely determined by some law of nature' (p. 312). But, if this is the case, it is also true that, for both, the encounter with such a law, with some kind of animating justice, involves not only knowing, but also unknowing. For both Hugo and Dostoyevsky, the capacity to imagine justice involves not only the assertion of a revolutionary ideal, but also the recognition that such ideals come to us not as revealed images, but as a radical failure of vision, of knowledge, and of the law. It may be that, as the revolutionary visionary Enjolras puts it in *Les Misérables*, we are 'aiming' for that perfect coincidence of law with justice that we find in utopian fictions from More onwards. Just as, in More's text, there is no need for an oppressive legal code because justice is already present in nature – is already 'simple and apparent' to all those who look for it[9] – so the revolutionaries in Hugo's text demand the end of the state-administered law and call for a law which enforces itself by natural justice. 'What are we aiming at?', Enjolras asks his comrades on the barricades: 'At government by knowledge, with the nature of things the only social force, natural law containing its penalties and sanctions within itself, and based on its evident truth: a dawn of truth corresponding to the laws of daylight' (p. 1004). This is truth that has a 'clear light shin[ing] through it', truth perfectly unified with the natural laws that express it. But the contradiction that runs through *Les Misérables*, as it runs through *Crime and Punishment*, is that this perfect coincidence of true justice and the law is imaginable only through the failure of the forms we have available in which to imagine it. It is only as the law fails – as language fails to capture the truth that animates it, and as the novel reveals its 'insubstantiality' – that the ideal asserts itself as a latent element within the real.

Two key passages in *Les Misérables*, which have their counterparts in *Crime and Punishment*, will serve to demonstrate this contradiction. The first comes as Jean Valjean, freed after a nineteen-year imprisonment for stealing a loaf of bread, finds himself committing a second crime – a crime born from his deep resentment at the injustice of his original punishment, and a crime for which the police inspector Javert relentlessly pursues him over the remaining chapters of the novel. This second crime, like the first, is a petty one. Valjean steals a forty sous piece from a small boy whom he meets on the road, by trapping the coin under his foot when the boy drops it, and then refusing to give it back when the boy pleads with him to do so. This is a petty crime, but everything that happens in the novel emerges, in a sense, from the dynamics that this crime puts in motion. As Valjean commits this act of cruel unkindness he is in the process of a moral awakening – forging that passage from injustice to justice, from falsity to truth, that the narrator associates with the emergence of French revolutionary consciousness. Just before Valjean encounters the boy on the road, an act of great kindness had been bestowed upon him. A Bishop took him in for the night and showed him hospitality and forgiveness, with an unconditional generosity that makes Valjean suddenly, confusedly aware of the possibility of unclouded good in the world. As he lays his foot upon the boy's coin, he is thus in a peculiar state of moral transition. The foot that he places on the coin belongs to the man that Valjean used to be, the brutal, vengeful convict who has been punished relentlessly and with ferocious injustice for a petty crime committed out of desperate poverty. The man who he is in the process of becoming, who has been made possible by the Bishop's act of kindness and generosity, has not yet come fully into existence. As the boy struggles with Valjean to recover his coin, trying to prise the convict's leaden foot from the ground, the prose registers this strange gap between the Valjean of the past and the Valjean of the future. 'The boy seized hold of his collar and shook him', the narrator says, 'while at the same time he tried to shift the heavy, iron-studded shoe covering his coin' (p. 113). Valjean's foot takes on an extraordinary dead weight here, as it belongs to the brute body that the transformed Valjean no longer occupies. Neither the boy nor Valjean himself can move this heavy, iron-studded foot, because this moment in the novel sees a great gulf opening between the material body, plunged in the heavy clay of reality, and the weightless movement of the nascent, emergent conscience. The moral sense that is being born within Valjean does not yet have either a material or a linguistic form in which it might express itself, and so is manifest only in a kind of stupefaction, a kind of dumb absence from self. 'In simple terms', Hugo's narrator explains, 'it was not the man who had stolen; it was the animal which, from habit and instinct, had brutally set its foot on the coin while the man's intelligence wrestled with the new and dumbfounding thoughts that preoccupied it' (p. 117). The prospect of justice which opens itself to Valjean here – the possibility of a 'life of goodness and purity' (p. 116) that an act of unbounded kindness makes suddenly imaginable to him – is absolutely not one which comes to him as a fully formed revelation. Rather, the kind of transfiguration that the contemplation of justice causes in him is one which disassembles him, casts him into a state of unknowing in which the bonds that hold him in his body, the ties that bind justice to the laws by which it is known, are broken rather than in any way strengthened or established. 'The fact is', the narrator says, 'that in robbing the boy he had committed an act of which he was no longer capable' (p. 117). In committing this crime, Valjean lives out a contradiction between the material and the ideal, the body and the emerging soul, the future and the past; a contradiction that is at the heart of Hugo's analysis of revolutionary possibility. Revolutions do not occur when justice makes itself known, but, rather, when the forces that bind us to ourselves, that make us responsible for our own actions, are suspended, and when an element of the unknown, the impossible, the unthought, enters into our most intimate relations with ourselves and with others.

The second passage that I want to look at from *Les Misérables* might appear to be the mirror image of the first. This passage turns not around the process by which an emerging consciousness reaches towards an unwritten justice, but rather around the way that the law itself responds to such an emergence; and it has as its protagonist not the just criminal Valjean, but the criminally just Javert. Javert, in chasing Valjean with a kind of demented obsessiveness, comes to represent the inflexibility of the law, the perception that the legal forms in which justice is coded must always in some sense deface the justice they set out to enshrine. Javert, the narrator says, is the 'personification of justice, light, and truth in their sublime task of stamping out evil' (p. 267). His faith in the law is such that he can admit of no nuance, no scenario in which the law might be out of step with justice, in which one's ethical duty might require one to breach the law oneself. His determination to capture and punish Valjean for a crime against the letter but not the spirit of the law thus makes Javert himself a kind of criminal, one who has a 'countenance on which was inscribed all the evil in what is good' (p. 268). Indeed, the terms in which the narrator imagines Javert's administering of ruthless justice reflect exactly the kind of stupefied violence that characterises Valjean's crime itself. As Valjean steps upon the boy's forty sous piece, so Javert seeks to 'stamp' upon petty criminality. 'He was setting his foot in righteous indignation upon crime', the narrator says, and 'was smiling with satisfaction as he did' (p. 267). But the passage I have in mind here is the one in which, late in the book, Javert is finally forced to acknowledge that the law, in serving justice, has to be prepared to annihilate itself, to demolish itself in attempting to answer to a truth that remains beyond its reach. If Javert, throughout the book, shares with Sherlock Holmes a sense that the law is an infallible machine, that the elimination of the impossible or the deviant or the criminal must always lead to the discovery of truth, here, at the close of the book, he recognises that the law is sometimes the casualty of truth rather than its guardian, that justice is the very province of the impossible and the unknowable, rather than its antidote. Javert finally captures Valjean, but only at that climactic moment in the book when he recognises that it is his duty to let him go, the moment when Valjean's passage towards justice coincides with the law's recognition of its own fallibility, the moment when Javert's mechanical 'pincer' becomes 'a hand with fingers that parted' (p. 1107) (a transformation of iron pincer into living fingers that signifies also the final lifting of Valjean's inhuman mechanical foots inhuman mechanical foot). 'Until now', Javert thinks as he reflects upon his decision to release Valjean, he 'had been conscious of nothing unknowable'. The 'unexpected, the glimpse of chaos,' he goes on, 'these belonged to some unknown, recalcitrant, miserable world'. But the recognition that Valjean could both be a criminal and a saviour, could transgress and redeem himself at the same time, forces Javert into 'confronting the unknown', into acknowledging that there 'were cases when the law, mumbling excuses, must bow to transfigured crime' (p. 1107). The acknowledgement costs Javert his life; he cannot live in a world where 'true fact should wear so distorted a face'. 'If facts did their duty', Javert thinks, 'they would simply reinforce the law' (p. 1108). But they do not, he realises. It may be the case that we are bound into the things of the world which are ruled by physical laws, which have an unflinching duty to be as they are. We are bound to matter as Valjean is bound to his iron foot. But this moment in the novel is one in which Javert recognises that matter is also inhabited by the unknown, by that 'indistinctness' without which, as Elizabeth Bowen puts it, 'things do not exist'. There is no law that can govern this indistinctness, he recognises, and so the only response to a justice that resides within such chaos, within such dark unknowing, is for the law itself, like Javert, to commit suicide, to bow silently to transfigured crime.

Taken together, these two passages enact the contradiction between the substantial and the insubstantial, between justice and the law, that runs not only through *Les Misérables*, but through the nineteenth-century novel of crime and punishment more generally. Dostoyevsky's *Crime and Punishment*, a novel which owes a great debt to *Les Misérables*, is similarly concerned with the possibility that crime might transfigure, that the law cannot simply enshrine justice but must also somehow give way before it. Dostoevsky's

Raskolnikov, like Hugo's Valjean, feels his way towards a new future by overcoming or setting himself against established norms and protocols. Just as Valjean feels 'quite unable to account for what was taking place within him' (p. 115), as the Bishop introduces him to the possibility of goodness, so Dostoyevsky's novel is propelled by Raskolnikov's feeling that 'something new seemed to be accomplishing itself within him' (p. 14), the emergence of a new self for which he has no language and no form. And for Raskolnikov, as in a different way for Valjean, this encountering of a new condition involves the breaking of the law – in Raskolnikov's case the brutal and unprovoked murder of an innocent woman. It is only in the commission of such a terrible crime, Raskolnikov believes – only in crossing the far horizon of established rules of normalcy and decency – that one can gain any purchase on the established rules themselves. The 'extraordinary' person, he says, who seeks to understand the rules governing existence, has to be able to transgress them, has a 'right, not an official right, of course, but a private one, to allow his conscience to step across certain . . . obstacles' (p. 308). And as Raskolnikov transgresses these norms, steps across these obstacles, he discovers, like Javert, that the law itself must give way before the unknown, before the 'chaos of existence' which is the nursery in which we formulate our idea of the world. The revolutionary, Raskolnikov suggests, is not one who brings truths into the light, but one who steps, himself, into the darkness; he or she is not an advocate of an existing justice, but a criminal who breaks the only laws by which justice is fleetingly known. All those who bring newness into the world, all 'who are capable of saying something new', he says, 'are bound, by their very nature, to be criminals'. There may be some 'law of nature' that 'governs the way in which people come into the world', but, Raskolnikov says, the only thing we can be sure of is that 'this law' is 'at present unknown to us' (p. 312). In order to reach for it, to divine it, we must transgress those laws that we do know. For the law to reach towards the justice that we don't yet understand it has to annihilate itself. The criminal revolutionary is thus committed to 'the destruction of the present reality in the name of one that is better' (p. 310).

So, both Hugo and Dostoyevksy live out the struggle at the heart of the nineteenth-century novel, between justice and law, between the written and the unwritten. But if *Les Misérables* and *Crime and Punishment* seem in a sense to be doing something very similar, it is also the case that most accounts of literary history would suggest that the passage from the former to the latter, from Hugo to Dostoyevsky, sees a seismic transformation in the very foundations of the novel form. The relationship between the two writers might be seen as a kind of hinge that connects the novel of social and psychological realism (reaching back through Austen and Gaskell to Burney, Swift and Defoe) to the novel of alienated modernity (reaching forward to Joyce, Woolf, Kafka and Stein). Where Hugo's novel, as Nathalie Babel Brown puts it, might be seen as a 'social novel of public activism', Dostoyevsky's novel tends to undermine the very terms upon which social activism is based. 'Hugo's work', Brown writes, enabled 'a century of social protest', while 'Dostoyevsky's prefigured the aliena-tion of modern man'.[10] In Hugo's novel, even as the revolutionary spirit disrupts the laws by which society is governed, it remains the case, as the narrator puts it, that 'matter exists, and the moment exists' (p. 1048). The pursuit of justice means that spirit moves in matter, that 'matter is the starting point, and the point of arrival is the soul' (1049); but the realist surface of Hugo's work remains pecu-liarly robust, maintaining its investment in the primacy of matter as the basis of collective life. Its own formal depiction of the space and time within which revolutionary action might take place remains largely untroubled by such action. Indeed, its effectiveness as a 'novel of public activism' is perhaps dependent upon its capacity to maintain a picture of a public sphere which has great spatial and temporal unity and coherence. For Dostoyevsky, however, the recog-nition that the search for justice necessitates the 'destruction of the present reality' involves an aesthetic as well as a philosophical encounter with formlessness, with the failure of existing protocols of realism. If Dostoyevsky 'prefigure[s] the alienation of modern man', he does so perhaps because his novels play out the impact that a kind of revolutionary nihilism has on our capacity to maintain collective pictures of the world. It is easy to see how Dostoyevsky's adaptation of the search for a revolutionary justice in Hugo leads us away from the forms of social realism that characterise the earlier nineteenth-century novel and towards the kinds of modernist experimentation that mark the end of the nineteenth century and the beginning of the twentieth. It is the pressure that Dostoyevsky applies to Hugo's model of prose realism, this kind of argument goes, that takes us towards the 'rejection of reality' that a critic such as Lukács finds in the works of Kafka, Beckett, Joyce and Woolf. The shift away from social realism towards modern alienation enacted in the passage from *Les Misérables* to *Crime and Punishment* leads towards a modernism in which nothingness is no longer involved in a dialectical struggle with matter. Dostoyevsky's adaptation of Hugo's realism leads us to the 'transcendent Nothingness' that Lukács finds in Kafka, a kind of Blanchottian insubstantiality in which 'non-existence is the ground of all existence'.[11]

There is no doubt some truth to this account of literary history. But I think also that our understanding of the broader literary historical passage of the modern novel – from the satirical enlightenment rationalism of Swift and Voltaire, through the development of nineteenth-century social and psychological realism, to the emergence of modernism and then of postmodernism – has tended to blind us to the possibility that, beneath these shifting historical forms, the novel is bound by a kind of formal genetics, a genotype that underlies the phenotypical expressions of historical difference. What I have argued in this book so far is that, beneath the historical distinctions that operate between, say, Beckett and Dickens, or between George Eliot and Zadie Smith, one can find something like a novel imagination, a fictional logic that binds these writers, despite their differences. And here I think it is the case that, even as Dostoyevsky offers a kind of bridge that takes us from the social realism of Hugo to the modernism of Kafka, it is important to realise that Hugo, Dostoyevsky and Kafka are all involved in a kind of imaginative work that is native to the novel itself. The critical emphasis on the capacity of modernist writing to ground itself in non-existence – whether it meets the disapproval of social realists such as Lukács or the enthusiasm of modernists such as Blanchot – has tended to elide the fact that, in modernism as in nineteenth-century realism, the very possibility of the novel emerges from its capacity to capture and express a dialectical relationship between the existent and the non-existent, between Flaubert's 'matter' and 'nothingness', between Gertrude's 'art' and 'matter'. If we are to understand the capacity of the novel to articulate a kind of justice – if we are to understand how the novel has a particular gift for ethical thinking – it is this common investment in the relationship between art and matter that we need to address.

Indeed, it is perhaps in Kafka's work, as the historical current takes us from the realist to the abstract, that the struggle between the existent and the non-existent that is so central to the novel's imagining of crime and punishment reaches its greatest intensity. This struggle, and this intensity, has been difficult to articulate in relation to Kafka, in part because of the dominant critical attitudes to the idealism of modernist art. Lukács makes an exemplary claim when he writes that 'the supreme judges in *The Trial*, the castle administration in *The Castle*, represent transcendence in Kafka's allegories'.[12] These administrators of justice, Lukács argues, are at once all powerful, and entirely non-existent. 'Everything points to them', he writes, 'and they could give meaning to everything. Everybody believes in their existence and omnipotence; but nobody knows them, nobody knows how they can be reached'. Kafka imagines a world driven by a set of legal apparatuses that have no actual existence, and, in so doing, Lukács argues, he suggests that the world itself is based on a kind of epistemological and ethical emptiness, a foundational vacuum which undermines the reality that it governs. 'The doings of this bureaucracy', Lukács goes on, 'and of those dependent on it, its impotent victims, are not concrete and realistic, but a reflection of the Nothingness which governs existence' (p. 44). Lukács' conception of modernism, as a rejection of the terms upon which social realism is based, leads him to regard Kafka's investment in nothingness, emptiness and non-existence as an abdication of the political duty of art to imagine better worlds. Real existence, Lukács suggests, breaks away from the non-existence imagined in the artwork – Blanchot's 'insubstantiality' – and so Kafka's works themselves become about nothing, can only live out the artwork's own absence of meaning. 'Kafka is not able', Lukács writes, 'to achieve that fusion of the particular and the general which is the essence of realistic art' (p. 45).

Lukács' reading of Kafka, though, is I think extraordinarily blind to the obsession with the materiality of existence that runs throughout his fiction, and as a result is blind as well to the ethical charge of Kafka's encounter with the non-existent. It is not the case, I would argue, that Kafka cannot create that 'fusion' of the particular and the general, the concrete and the abstract, that Lukács finds in 'realistic art'; or, more accurately, the difficulty of this kind of 'fusion' is as much a preoccupation for Kafka as it is for any of his realist predecessors. The archetypal scenario in Kafka is one in which a body finds itself immersed in an overwhelmingly material space that is governed by a set of rules that are everywhere manifest, but which cannot come to any focus or clarity. Think of Gregor Samsa, incarcerated in the hideous body of an insect, or K. laboriously tramping through the heavy snow in a vain attempt to reach the Castle, or the opening scene of *The Trial*, in which K. is put under arrest. In the latter, as two agents of the law arrive to arrest K., the focus is immediately trained on the effect that this unaccountable arrest has on K.'s body, on his freedom of movement. As one of the 'warders' tells K. that 'you are not allowed to go from here', that 'you are after all under arrest', K. feels the arrest as a physical force exerted upon him. 'He made', the narrator says, 'an abrupt movement as if he were tearing himself free from the two men who were in fact standing some distance away from him'.[13] The trial to which K. is subjected, however notional, however abstract, seems to him to exert a material pressure upon him, 'as if his freedom were being restricted, as if he were really being arrested' (p. 37). The claustrophobic effect of Kafka's writing arises from this intense focus on the experience of being in a body, of being plunged into one's material being, as Hugo's Valjean is plunged into his body when he lays his foot on the boy's forty sous piece. But this experience of embodied being is also and always an alienated one because, as Hugo finds, as Dostoyevsky finds, the law that governs it, that binds a striving consciousness to its material being, is 'at present unknown to us'. To think, in all three writers, is to encounter a justice that emerges from the unknown. There is no writer who is better than Kafka at capturing this disappearing movement of truth, as it simultaneously animates thought and withholds itself from it. K. struggles

with an extraordinarily impassioned earnestness to penetrate the law
that exercises itself upon him, and Kafka follows his attempt to *think*
the law with a shocking intimacy, as if working in the revealed insides
of our own striving minds, as if capturing and articulating that
strange vibration between knowing and unknowing that is the very
inward movement of thinking and being. As K. is arrested, the narrator
says, he 'wanted to worm his way somehow into the warders' minds',
to 'entrench himself' in their 'thoughts' (p. 5). But of course this
unbounded contact with the law is precisely what is not possible, in
art or in life. As K. ruefully puts it, echoing Dostoyevsky's
Raskolnikov, 'this law is unknown to me' (p. 5). But if Kafka gives an
unprecedentedly forceful expression to the unknowability of the law,
this does not mean that he is giving himself up in some sense to
Lukács' transcendental nothingness, or that he is abandoning the
concrete in favour of the abstract. Rather, in Kafka – as in
Dostoevsky, as in Hugo – nothingness, the unknown, is the province
of justice, the movement within the world of a truth that cannot come
fully to expression. If Kafka fails to achieve any kind of 'fusion'
between that truth and the material worlds to which his protagonists
are bound, this is not because he has given up on realism, or given up
on the real possibility of justice. Rather, the difficult striving for such
fusion – the promise that the ideal might be contained within the
material, combined with the endless revocation of this promise – is
the political reality that he addresses, as it is the reality addressed,
under different historical conditions, by Dostoyevksy, and by Hugo.

   This continual struggle between the material and the ideal as a
means of bringing justice to fictional expression is captured – in a way
that might help to bring both this chapter and this book to a close – in a
certain obsession that Kafka exhibits in *The Trial* with lips. If Kafka is
fascinated by the material occupation of the body – by the forces which
hold us within our flesh – then this fascination is drawn in particular to
those surfaces, often erogenous, at which the borders of the body seem
most open. K.'s whole body becomes an almost unbearably erotic
surface his skin glistens with an irresistible beauty – but the part of
his body that becomes the most powerful site of such peculiar, charged
eroticism is his mouth, and in particular his lips. His neighbour Fraulein

Montag, for example, cannot take her eyes off K.'s lips throughout their conversations with each other. They have a number of excruciating encounters, in which, as so often in Kafka, the central burden of the conversation seems elusive, seems not quite to resolve itself to clear, non-contradictory expression ('that's true', Fraulein Montag will say, 'or rather, that's not how it is at all' (p. 63)), and in the midst of one of these talks, K. thinks to himself that he is 'tired of seeing Fraulein Montag staring at his lips all the time' (p. 63). Now, in a sense this distracting attention to his lips is an effect of K.'s sexual allure. One feels that Fraulein Montag has fallen under his spell, captured by the strange aura that, K.'s advocate later claims, makes 'all accused men' appear 'handsome' (p. 144). But if the magnetism of K.'s lips is erotic in nature, it also has to do with the novel's obsessive concern with the capacity for our bodies, our speech, to capture some element of truth – the capacity for the abstract truth to be contained in material form. It is perhaps for this reason that it is the open borders of the body – the lips, the eyes, the ears – that are at the centre of Kafka's obsessive gaze. Fraulein Montag is staring at K.'s lips, he thinks to himself, not because she is longing to kiss him – or not only so – but because 'she was trying by this means to assume control of whatever he might say' (p. 63). Just as K. longs to 'worm his way into the warders' thoughts', to somehow leap from his own body into theirs, to penetrate into the heart of what it is they are thinking, so, he imagines, Fraulein Montag is interested in his lips not only as erogenous surfaces, but also as legible ones – as the fleshy portals through which meaning might pass from one mind to another. If, as J.M. Coetzee puts it in *Elizabeth Costello*, Kafka's work marks a moment in the history of literary expression at which words 'will no longer stand up and be counted, each proclaiming "I mean what I mean"',[14] then this fascination with the lips as the organs of speech is perhaps a despairing mark of such failure. In staring at K.'s lips, Fraulein Montag is seeking to discover an attachment between words and things, between who we are and what we say, an attachment which seems in *The Trial* to have been cancelled, to have become esoteric or estranged.

As this fascination with lips reaches out across the novel, the sense that language and the body has come asunder, that meaning is no longer properly contained within the forms that express it, only becomes more powerful, more disturbing. Much later in the novel, K. has an excruciating interview with an Italian banker whom it is his job to impress. As so often in this novel, this meeting is oddly overwritten with a kind of dream logic, making the details of the scene seem unhinged, out of joint. The Italian, for example, has a 'steely-grey bushy moustache', which was 'evidently scented', and which 'K. felt tempted to go up close and smell' (p. 156). This might be a recognisable dream scenario, laden with skewed desire; but when the Italian starts speaking, the dream quickens into nightmare. K. realises, as soon as he tries to communicate with him, that 'he understood the Italian only fragmentarily', that 'the words simply poured out of his mouth and he kept shaking his head as if this delighted him' (p. 156). This scenario, in which language becomes strangely empty, a cascade of faulty words in which something can at once be 'true' and 'not how it is at all', is of course the central predicament of the novel, and as K. struggles to understand, to convert this logorrhoetic stream of sound into sense, he finds himself in precisely Fraulein Montag's position. He tries to watch the Italian's lips – seeking 'by this means to assume control of whatever he might say' – but finds that he can't quite focus properly on his mouth, because of that peculiar, alluringly scented moustache. 'K. saw that there was little likelihood that he could communicate with the Italian', the narrator says, because 'the moustache concealed the lip movements which might have helped K. understand' (p. 156).

Throughout *The Trial*, and indeed across his entire oeuvre, Kafka has made of this odd dislocation, this eerie and compelling separation between words and what they mean, an intoxicating and utterly singular kind of poetry. To read Kafka is to fall, with a strange, suicidal joy, into this gulf. But, as I have argued in various ways throughout this book, the estrangement that we find in Kafka – the estranged tongue that is the native language of the novel – does not spell anything like an abandonment of a struggle towards meaning, truth or justice. To give expression to the empty space between language and the world, to try to live in this suspended interval, is not, *absolutely not*, to give oneself up to a 'transcendent nothingness'. It is, rather, to reach for a form in which to conceive *Hamlet*'s 'nothing' that is 'more than matter',[15] the nothingness that Flaubert tries to capture in his material imagination, the nothingness that is not the absence of justice, but its guarantee, the condition of its possibility. To write one's way to this emptiness is not the failure of realism, but, as Hugo puts it in *Les Misérables*, is the very aim of realism itself – that 'process of burrowing', he writes, which 'takes us past the borderline separating the indistinct from the invisible' (p. 620, 621). To move towards a justice that inhabits the world but that does not yet have a language in which to express itself, one must make one's home in the invisible, in those seams of disappearance that are shot through George Eliot's prose, that it is the task of the novel to mine. It is in these seams – the 'lower galleries', Hugo writes, 'that are everywhere mined and tunnelled' – that we find the trace of justice, the trace of the future. It is as the novel takes us towards the invisible – as, in Eliot's phrase, it 'threads the hidden pathways of thought'[16] – that we might see the darkness in which the future is hidden, that we might become, as Hugo puts it, 'confusedly aware of shadowy figures that perhaps do not yet exist' (p. 620).

The moment in *The Trial* at which this possibility rises closest to the surface comes, unsurprisingly, as K. finds himself drawn towards his death – and it comes also at the moment when the novel's obsession with lips reaches a sort of conclusion. In a late conversation with the merchant Block, K. is given a kind of key that explains why so many people, not just Fraulein Montag, have been obsessed with his lips. There is a commonly held superstition, Block tells K., that 'the outcome of a case can be seen in the accused man's face, and particularly in the line of his lips' (p. 136). If K.'s lips are particularly striking, then this is because they are a sign of his guilt, of his impending conviction. It has been said, Block goes on, that 'judging by your lips, you are sure to be convicted, and soon' (p. 136). At this point, the ideas that have floated around an absent centre in *The Trial*, that have connected lips with a strange, displaced desire, and with the missing conjunction between meaning and language, are given a new kind of shape; it is the missing, unknown justice that moves through *The Trial*, Block suggests, that might bring the displaced psychic elements of which the novel is made into a new alignment, that might make one's lips, the very expression on the face, once more transparent and legible. K.'s response to this information is perhaps the moment in the novel of the highest pathos. 'My lips?', K. repeats, 'taking out a pocket mirror and examining himself. 'I can't see anything peculiar about my lips, can you?'(p. 136). This glance in the mirror is freighted with myth. It is surely Narcissus regarding himself in the lake, surely the mark of K.'s ageless obsession with self. But it is also, oddly, the moment in the novel when the desperate search for a meaningful communication with others – a communication conducted under the sign of some kind of ethical truth, some kind of justice – is at its purest. *The Trial* responds to the perception that we are plunged in our bodies, without an adequate means of understanding what such immurement means. The desires that move and torment us, the longing for company, for truth, for love, are all driven by an agent force which withholds itself from us. As K. looks anxiously at his lips, he is looking for that absent agency, a manifest sign of that force that binds us to ourselves and to others, thinking, in a deranged way, that it might suddenly reveal itself to him.

In the days that *The Trial* first began to formulate itself in Kafka's mind, he wrote in his diary that he was 'ready to carry on a conversation with myself',[17] and this moment in the novel is when this conversation comes closest to taking place. K.'s nervous glance in the mirror speaks of his recognition that the question of his innocence or guilt – the question that hangs over the entire novel – requires this kind of address, this new encounter with oneself. If we are to know our own innocence, if we are to understand what is required of us, and whether we have answered this demand, it is this kind of scrutiny of the self that is required. Of course, whatever justice might animate the law in *The Trial* never does make itself known, and the law before which we are held accountable remains cruel, arbitrary, stupid. But, as K. meets his death, the possibilities held in that naked encounter with self – with self as other – return, graced by a kind of unlit utopian promise. As K. is put to death, he is granted the prospect of a mute encounter with another, like that wordless encounter that Mrs Dalloway has with her elderly neighbour at the climactic scene of *Mrs Dalloway*, an encounter which takes place in the empty space where justice, in its very absence, might yet be found. He can see a 'human figure, faint and insubstantial', standing 'at a casement window', and as the knife is turned in his heart, this figure comes closer and closer, until, 'with his failing sight', K. sees him 'right in front of his face, cheek pressed against his cheek' (p. 176). This is the shared moment that the novel sets out to produce, the intimate encounter with another who is pressed right close against us; but it is also the final throes of that 'conversation' that both K. and Kafka set out here to have with themselves. K.'s final thought is a 'thankful' one; he is 'thankful', he thinks, 'that they've left it to me to say what has to be said to myself' (p. 176). There is no final word of God in this novel, no revelation; justice does not come out of hiding, the future does not arrive, ahead of schedule. But what this novel does – what, I think *the* novel does – is to open this space between self and self, between self and other, where the possibility of truth and justice resides, the possibility that makes everything matter, without becoming itself matter. It is the conversation that K. has with himself in this novel that brings this nothing that is more than matter to the trembling brink of the thinkable. The demand that we encounter this nothing, that we try to think it, that is the law of the novel, and its truth.

Conclusion: The Thing Which Is Not

Do thou, too, live in this world without being of it.

Herman Melville, *Moby Dick*.[1]

In a 2014 article entitled 'The Novel is Dead (this time it's for real)', Will Self offers a typically witty and trenchant account of the future of the novel – or the perceived lack thereof. The novel is a product of a certain period of modernity, Self argues, and a certain conception of the relationship between the private individual and the public sphere. The experiments that we associate with modernism – 'the telescoping of fictional characters into their streams of consciousness; the abandonment of the omniscient narrator; the inability to suspend disbelief in the artificialities of plot' – are symptoms, for Self, of the slow malfunctioning of the apparatuses of the novel.[2] Joyce's *Finnegans Wake*, he suggests, marks the moment at which the 'form should have been laid to rest'. There have been 'many fine novels written' in the period after Joyce's late experiments in narrative, but, Self writes, these are 'zombie novels, instances of an undead art form that yet wouldn't lie down'.

Self offers two reasons for this extended death of the novel in the aftermath of Joycean modernism, both of which are connected to the emergence of electronic communication. The first has to do with the experience of a certain cultural exhaustion, a sense that, with the access to the entire archive of human expression provided by the internet, there comes a failure of our capacity to imagine anything original, to create anything different or surprising. 'The instant availability of almost everything that had ever been done', Self writes, has the effect of 'stifling creativity' and locking us into a 'permanent now', a condition in which everything is available, so nothing either ages or strikes us as new. The second reason that Self gives follows on from the first: if the electronic media that developed over the twentieth century allow us access to the past, to the archive, they also offer us unbroken access to each other. The experience of hyperconnectivity that comes with the emergence of the internet leads to the loss of any kind of privacy, any sense that we can withdraw from the public sphere, into some inner space of contemplation or thought. 'I've come to realise', Self writes, 'that the kind of psyche implicit in the production and consumption of serious novels depends on a medium that has inbuilt privacy'. As Dave Eggers' novel *The Circle* amply demonstrates, the emergence of the electronic public sphere crowds out that privacy, the 'few cubic centimetres inside your skull' that George Orwell's Winston Smith cherishes as a place of sanctuary from the surveillance technology employed by the thought police.[3] The collapse of the formal mechanisms of the novel, the loss of the omniscient narrator, the folding of narrative into stream of consciousness, the failure of a believable plot, all follow, Self suggests, from the disappearance of the boundary between the democratic public sphere, and the private, reflective mind – the boundary upon which the cultures of modernity rested, and the boundary which the production of a new electronic public sphere has more or less entirely erased. The novel belonged to a period in which the imagining mind was able to craft forms of refuge and retreat from the collective world – forms of withdrawal in which one could contemplate the terms in which one belonged to the body politic. As the world has appeared increasingly to swamp the mind, the literary novel entered first into those experiments with private consciousness that we associate with modernism, and is now in the process of fading away altogether, leaving the field open for a new form, as yet unimagined, which will be better suited to making critical pictures of our newly unified culture.

The novel has been accompanied, throughout its history, by tracts, such as Self's, which prophecy its imminent demise; Self's subtitle is an acknowledgement of this critical tradition. And each time that this kind of prediction is made, it has a certain plausibility.

The novel today does feel precarious, like its own afterimage or zombie avatar – 'serious fiction' now does seem to exceed its own conditions of possibility. But what Self's essay tends to overlook, like those other 'death of the novel' essays that came before it, is that this precarity is not a mark of the failure of the novel, not a sign of its demise, but the very condition of its being. Self's nostalgia for the world to which the novel seemed to him to belong – and the connected tendency to resist the new forms of democracy enabled by contemporary information technology – is based, I think, on a partial understanding of the way that the novel has historically negotiated the claims of collective life, and of how such claims impact upon the freedom of the mind to contemplate its own singularity, its freedom from an archive of knowledge or from a community of other thinkers. The novel has come into being, I have argued throughout this book, in the teeth of a contradiction between the desire for collective belonging – for the possibility of a fully realised democratic condition in which the law achieves a perfect accord with abstract conceptions of the justice and the good – and the refusal of such collective forms, the struggle towards a private or withheld or non-existent space in which the mind might encounter itself outside of the conditions determined by existing cultural forms. This struggle has always been difficult, and always led the novel to confront its own disappearance, to stage its own becoming as a denial of the zeitgeist. To see the death of the novel that arises from the advent of communication technology as a singular event – to claim, as Self does in his parenthetical subtitle, that this death is the 'real' one – is to fail to see that the novel has always risked its own death as part of its struggle to live. The novelist, as Beckett puts it in an epitaph he composed early in his career, has 'so hourly died that he lived on till now'.[4]

The novel in which this contradiction is given perhaps the sharpest expression – and from which I take the title of this conclusion – comes, accordingly, quite early in the history of the modern form. In the final book of Jonathan Swift's *Gulliver's Travels*, 'A Voyage to the Houyhnhnms', Gulliver travels to a land ruled by horses ('Houyhnhnms'), in which humans (or 'Yahoos') are the beasts of burden. Swift represents this land as a kind of utopia, and Gulliver himself is entranced by the perfection of the Houyhnhnms, by their Apollonian grace and serene rationality. As with More's utopia, and most utopias that come after him, in Swift's depiction of a perfect state we see the arrival of revealed and established truth, the truth brought out of hiding. There is no need for law, or punishment, or the exercise of state power, because the Houyhnhnms have discovered a mode of life in which reason and nature perfectly coincide, in which one is *led* to do, by one's own instinct and inclination, what one *must* do in accordance with the public good. In the land of the Houyhnhnms there is no distinction between private desire and public good, because the grounds of this distinction – the very possibility that one's private thoughts or inclinations might be at odds with the requirements of the state – have been abolished. In the land of the Houyhnhnms, the loss of privacy dreaded by Self has already arrived. Indeed, their language reflects this loss, this sense that deviance, discord or any kind of difference between the self and the state, has been overcome. Gulliver tries to explain European culture to his Houyhnhnm 'master' – to give him 'some idea' of the 'desire of power', the 'terrible effects of Lust, Intemperance, Malice and Envy' that obtains there[5] – but the Houyhnhnm, for all his intelligence, finds it very difficult to grasp such horrors. He can hardly conceive of such things, Gulliver says, because 'Power, Government, War, Law, Punishment, and a Thousand other things had no Terms wherein that language could express them' (p. 236). Their existence in the light of truth and reason is so complete, in fact, that they even have no conception of what it would be to lie, to dissemble, to experience any kind of disjunction between what they say and what they mean. The Houyhnhnms believe, like the architects of the 'Communications 101' handbook in J.M. Coetzee's novel *Disgrace*, that 'the Use of Speech was to make us understand one another, and to receive Information of Facts'. To lie, to *'say the Thing which was not'* (p. 232), would be perversely to cast oneself out of the light of such communication, such community – a kind of self-extinction that the Houyhnhnms, rational creatures as they are, cannot contemplate.

Swift, of course, intends this picture of the perfect Houyhnhnms as a satire. Gulliver becomes infatuated with the horses, to the extent that when he arrives back home at the end of the novel, he won't condescend to speak to any of his fellow Yahoos, walks with a fussy little trot and speaks with a kind of neigh. The bite of the satire is perhaps to suggest that the bid for perfection, the search for a fully enlightened consciousness, leads only to absurdity. But the beauty of Swift's novel, and the challenge it presents to interpretation, is that it continually invests in those principles that it satirises and continually destabilises and bends those positions and rhetorical forms that it seeks to uphold. One cannot read this novel without recognising that the forms of democratic perfection that the Houyhnhnms represent are a real object of aesthetic and political desire. The novel is charged with a bitter dissatisfaction with the faulty democracies of eighteenth-century Europe, and with a real longing for a form of civic good that is in part represented by the inhabitants of Houyhnhnm land. But the longing for this form of political good, as More finds in his picture of Utopia, can only come into being in the form of a fantasy, of a *fiction*, which draws attention continually to its own non-being. The Houyhnhnms' bar on lying, on saying *the thing which was not*, is of course a prohibition of fiction itself, which carries an echo of Plato's *Republic*. If we were to live in the land of the Houyhnhnms, we would not be able to conceive of a work of art such as *Gulliver's Travels*. In imagining the land of the Houyhnhnms, Swift is imagining a place where fiction would no longer be possible, a place in which we live content in the full ownership of our bodies, in which we know no lack and no difference from ourselves. The Houyhnhnms' knowledge of the true and the good is such that they live in complete accord with their bodies, experiencing that absolute match between body and self that Lawrence imagines in 'Why the Novel Matters', and that Gulliver himself so sorely misses as his body swells and shrinks, becoming strange and alien to itself. Because they 'live under the Government of reason', Gulliver writes, 'they are no more proud of the good Qualities they possess, than I should be for not wanting a Leg or an Arm' (p. 288). *Gulliver's Travels* is tuned to allow for this picture of unconscious accord with body, with state, with reason, but it produces this picture only by casting it in terms of the 'thing which was not', by representing it satirically. All we know about such perfection is that it is not here, it is not available. What the fictional imagination can do, uniquely, is summon the idea of such utopian harmony, while also producing a critical articulation of its absence, of its failure to arrive. It can make pictures of an achieved fullness of being while, in the same stroke, allowing a kind of negativity to stir within it, a kind of nothing, which is the only form that the ideal thing is able to take, here and now, when life is not yet over, reason has not yet become manifest and the meaning of the world remains a mystery to us.

It is this coming together of the good with the not – this conjunction between the capacity of the novel to cast pictures of collective life and its necessary failure to do so – that I have traced throughout this book. The novel, across its history, has allowed us to form pictures of bodies living collectively in spaces, under the authority of the law. I have tried here to capture some of the force of these pictures, the ways in which narrative allows us to conceive of living in regulated space and time. But, at every point, this book has suggested that the value of such picturing lies not only in its capacity to imagine community, but in its capacity to articulate a kind of emptiness at the heart of our life-worlds, a space where the thing itself is not, and where instead we might find the unpictured future, the latent possibility that is carried within the intrinsic indistinctness of the thing, its difference from itself. The novel, I think, is the form that is most able to instruct us, in Melville's words, on how to live in this world, without being of it; how to struggle with and against what we have and what we know, while also gearing ourselves to a future state which is not yet here. As we enter into the space and time of our immediate future, it is of course the case, as Will Self argues, that the space for withdrawal, the few cubic centimetres inside our skull, is likely to be compressed. We are living in the midst of an information revolution, and an eco-catastrophe, that will surely transform our relation both to the technosphere and to the biosphere. But for us to imagine that these transformations necessarily spell the death of the novel is to fail to see that the novel has always worked at the edge of the culture, in that space between a completely revealed world and a world that is yet to come. The novel is a kind of differential machine that is tuned to find the place, in the most revealed of utopias or in the most saturated and exhausted of cultures, where the thing which is not is concealed or secreted. The novel mines the seams of the latent and the unthought, as they work through the compacted material of the known. Under contemporary conditions, in which we are all summoned into new forms of community that are as potentially democratising as they are potentially tyrannical, it is the novel we need, more than ever, to help us to understand such communities and to live within them. It is the novel that might help us to frame the utopian potential of the world to come, while also preserving forms of withdrawal in which the thing that is not might live on, darkly lighting our way.

Notes

INTRODUCTION: THE VALUE OF THE NOVEL

1. Dave Eggers, *The Circle* (London: Penguin, 2014), p. 485.
2. Dorothy J. Hale, 'Aesthetics and the New Ethics: Theorizing the Novel in the Twenty-First Century', in *PMLA*, vol. 124, no. 3 (2009), p. 904.
3. For a recent critique of Eagleton's equivocation on this issue, to which my own argument here is indebted, see Andrew Hadfield, 'Turning Point: or, the wheel has come full circle', in *Textual Practice*, vol. 27, no. 1, pp. 1–8.
4. Terry Eagleton, *Literary Theory: An Introduction*, second edition (Oxford: Blackwell, 1996), p. 9.
5. See Terry Eagleton, *The Ideology of the Aesthetic* (Oxford: Blackwell, 1990).
6. Terry Eagleton, *How to Read Literature* (New Haven: Yale University Press, 2013), p. ix.
7. See Martha Nussbaum, *Not for Profit: Why Democracy Needs the Humanities* (New Jersey: Princeton University Press, 2010); Joshua Landy, *How to Do Things with Fictions* (Oxford: Oxford University Press, 2012); Lisa Zunshine, *Why We Read Fiction* (Columbus: Ohio State University Press, 2006); Sianne Ngai, *Ugly Feelings* (Cambridge: Harvard University Press, 2005); Helen Small, *The Value of the Humanities* (Oxford: Oxford University Press, 2013); Ray Ryan and Liam McIlvanney, *The Good of the Novel* (London: Faber and Faber, 2011).
8. See Mark McGurl, *The Program Era* (Cambridge: Harvard University Press, 2009). McGurl traces the growth of the US creative writing programme across the postwar decades, pointing out that in 1975 there were 52 creative writing programmes in the States, rising to 150 in 1984, and to more than 350 in 2004 (p. 24).

9. See John Guillory, *Cultural Capital: The Problem of Literary Canon Formation* (Chicago: University of Chicago Press, 1993).

10. J.M. Coetzee, *Disgrace* (London: Vinatge, 2000), p. 3.

11. Margaret Atwood, *Oryx and Crake* (London: Virago, 2009), p. 220.

12. Ronan McDonald, *The Death of the Critic* (London: Continuum, 2007), p. vii.

13. Don DeLillo, *Mao II* (London: Vintage, 1992), p. 157.

14. Philip Roth, *Exit Ghost* (London: Vintage, 2008), p. 181.

15. Samuel Beckett, *First Love*, in Samuel Beckett, *The Expelled and Other Novellas* (London: Penguin, 1980), p. 17.

16. I will be concerned here largely with the novel as it has developed since the early eighteenth century. But the novel form has been traced back, by critics such as Margaret Anne Doody, to ancient Greek, Roman and Chinese cultures, and emerges in many guises before its appearance as a dominant form in eighteenth century Europe (with what Franco Moretti calls 'The European Acceleration'). See Margaret Anne Doody, *The True Story of the Novel* (London: HarperCollins, 1997), and Franco Moretti ed., *The Novel*, 2 vols. (Princeton: Princeton University Press, 2006).

17. Nancy Armstrong, *How Novels Think: The Limits of Individualism from 1790–1900* (New York: Columbia University Press, 2005), p. 3.

18. McIlvanney and Ryan, *The Good of the Novel* (London: Faber and Faber, 2011), pp. viii, xiii.

19. Martha Nussbaum, *Love's Knowledge* (Oxford: Oxford University Press, 1990), p. 3.

I THE NOVEL VOICE

1. Sigmund Freud, *General Theory of the Neuroses*, in Sigmund Freud, *Introductory Lectures on Psychoanalysis* (Harmondsworth: Penguin, 1973), trans. James Strachey, p. 456.

2. Samuel Beckett, *Company*, in Samuel Beckett, *Nohow On* (London: Calder, 1992), p. 15.

3. George Eliot, *Daniel Deronda* (Oxford: Oxford University Press, 1988), p. 297.

4. Don DeLillo, *Underworld* (London: Picador, 1997), p. 11.

5. Michel Foucault, 'What Is an Author?', in Michel Foucault, *Language, Counter-Memory, Practice* (Oxford: Blackwell, 1977), ed. and trans. Donald F. Bouchard, p. 115.

6. Roland Barthes, 'The Death of the Author', in Roland Barthes, *Image – Music – Text* (Glasgow: Fontana, 1977), ed. and trans. Stephen Heath, p. 142.

7. Mladen Dolar, *A Voice and Nothing More* (Cambridge: The MIT Press, 2006), p. 37.

8. Andrew Gibson, '"And the Wind Wheezing through That Organ Once in a While"': Voice, Narrative, Film', in *New Literary History*, vol. 32, no. 3 (2001), p. 640.

9. Charles Dickens, *Bleak House* (Oxford: Oxford University Press, 1996), p. 24.

10. Charles Dickens, *David Copperfield* (London: Penguin, 2004), p. 33.

11. Samuel Beckett, *The Calmative*, in Samuel Beckett, *The Expelled and Other Novellas* (London: Penguin, 1980), p. 52.

12. Henry James, *Autobiography* (London: W.H. Allen, 1956), p. 68.

13. Samuel Beckett, *Molloy, Malone Dies, The Unnamable* (London: Calder 1994), p. 7.

14. J.M. Coetzee, *Doubling the Point: Essays and Interviews* (Cambridge: Harvard University Press, 1992), p. 231.

15. Monika Fludernik 'New Wine in Old Bottles?: Voice, Focalization, and New Writing', in *New Literary History* vol. 32, no. 3 (2001), p. 623.

16. Christine Brooke-Rose, 'Narrating Without a Narrator', in *The Times Literary Supplement*, 31 December 1999, p. 12.

17. Eliot, *Daniel Deronda*, p. 314.

18. Maurice Blanchot, *The Infinite Conversation* (Minneapolis: University of Minnesota Press 1993), trans. Susan Hanson, p. 329.

19. Beckett, *Malone Dies*, p. 195.

20. Beckett, *The Calmative*, p. 66.

21. Samuel Beckett, *Worstward Ho*, in Beckett, *Nohow On*, p. 119.

22. Samuel Beckett, *Texts for Nothing*, in Samuel Beckett, *The Complete Short Prose: 1929–1989* (New York: Grove Press, 1995), p. 103.

23. Dolar, *A Voice and Nothing More*, p. 103.

2   IS THIS REALLY REALISM?

1. Eliot, *Daniel Deronda*, p. 361.

2. Jacques Rancière, *The Emancipated Spectator* (London: Verso, 2009), p. 93.

3. Georg Lukács, *The Meaning of Contemporary Realism* (Monmouth: The Merlin Press, 2006), trans. John and Necke Mander, p. 48.

4. Fredric Jameson, *The Antinomies of Realism* (London: Verso, 2013), p. 3.

5. J.M. Coetzee, *Elizabeth Costello* (London: Viking, 2003), p. 18.

6. Zadie Smith, 'Two Directions for the Novel', in Zadie Smith, *Changing My Mind: Occasional Essays* (London: Penguin, 2011), p. 73.
7. See Peter Brooks, *Realist Vision* (New Haven: Yale University Press, 2005), p. 1, where Brooks writes that 'I think we have a thirst for reality'. See also David Shields, *Reality Hunger: A Manifesto* (London: Hamish Hamilton, 2010).
8. See Hal Foster, *The Return of the Real: The Avant-Garde at the End of the Century* (Cambridge: The MIT Press, 2001).
9. Ian Watt, *The Rise of the Novel* (Berkeley: University of California Press, 2001), p. 92.
10. J. Donald Crowley, 'Introduction', in Daniel Defoe, *Robinson Crusoe* (Oxford: Oxford University Press, 1983), p. xv.
11. Defoe, *Robinson Crusoe*, p. 64.
12. Dolar, *A Voice and Nothing More*, p. 83.
13. George Eliot, *Middlemarch* (London: Penguin, 1994), p. 194.
14. Dolar, *A Voice and Nothing More*, p. 83.

3 THE NOVEL BODY

1. Herman Melville, *Moby Dick* (Oxford: Oxford University Press, 1998).
2. Robert Louis Stevenson, *The Strange Case of Dr Jekyll and Mr Hyde* (London: Penguin, 2002), p. 68.
3. Beckett, *Worstward Ho*, p. 101.
4. Theodor Adorno, 'Commitment', in Ernst Bloch et al., *Aesthetics and Politics* (London: Verso, 1977), p. 178.
5. Elizabeth Bowen, 'Notes on Writing a Novel', in Elizabeth Bowen, *The Mulberry Tree* (London:Virago, 1986), p.39.
6. Thomas Bernhard, *Extinction* (London: Quartet, 1995), trans. David McLintock, p. 102.
7. Beckett, *Malone Dies*, p. 238.
8. Tom McCarthy, *Remainder* (London: Alma Books, 2011), p. 56.
9. Beckett, *The Calmative*, p. 51.
10. Samuel Beckett, *Watt* (London: Calder, 1976), p. 247.
11. Gustave Flaubert, *The Selected Letters of Gustave Flaubert* (London: Hamish Hamilton, 1954), trans. Francis Steegmuller, p. 131
12. Flaubert, *Selected Letters*, p. 131; Gustave Flaubert, *Correspondance* vol. II (Paris: Gallimard, 1980), p. 31.
13. James Wood, *The Broken Estate: Essays on Literature and Belief* (London: Pimlico, 2000), p. 54.

14. Judith Butler, *Bodies that Matter* (London: Routledge, 1993), p. 187.
15. Steven Connor, 'Thinking Things', in *Textual Practice*, vol. 24, no. 1 (2010), p. 1.
16. Donna J. Haraway, *Simians, Cyborgs, and Women: The Reinvention of Nature* (London: Free Association Books, 1991), p. 153.
17. See Alain Badiou, *The Rebirth of History: Times of Riots and Uprisings* (London: Verso, 2012).
18. Elaine Scarry, *Literature and the Body* (Baltimore: Johns Hopkins University Press, 1988), p. ix.
19. Jonathan Swift, *Gulliver's Travels* (Oxford: Oxford University Press, 1986), p. 7.
20. D.H. Lawrence, 'Why the Novel Matters', in D.H. Lawrence, *Study of Thomas Hardy, and Other Essays* (Cambridge: Cambridge University Press, 1985), ed. Bruce Steele, p. 195.
21. Scarry, *Literature and the Body*, p. vii.
22. Elizabeth Bowen, *The House in Paris* (London: Vintage, 1998), p. 117.
23. Louis Stevenson, *Jekyll and Hyde*, p. 75.
24. Bowen, *The House in Paris*, p. 119.
25. Herman Melville, *Moby Dick*, p. xliv; William Shakespeare, *King Henry IV* part 1, 1.3.56.
26. Patrick McGrath, 'Introduction to *Moby Dick*', in Harold Bloom, *Herman Melville's Moby Dick* (New York: Infobase, 2007), p. 21.
27. Eliot, *Middlemarch*, p. 165.

4 MAKING TIME MATTER

1. Don DeLillo, *The Body Artist* (London: Picador, 2001), p. 92.
2. Paul Ricoeur, *Time and Narrative*, vol. 1, trans. Kathleen McLaughlin and David Pellauer (Chicago: University of Chicago Press, 1984), p. 3.
3. H.G. Wells, *The Time Machine*, in H.G. Wells, *Selected Short Stories* (Harmondsworth: Penguin, 1958), p. 7.
4. Sir Arthur Eddington, *Space, Time and Gravitation: An Outline of the General Theory of Relativity* (Cambridge: Cambridge University Press, 1920), p. 57.
5. Saint Augustine, *Confessions* (London: Penguin, 1961), trans. R.S. Pine-Coffin, p. 264.
6. Bowen, *The House in Paris*, p. 62.
7. C.F.G. Masterman, *In Peril of Change: Essays Written in Time of Tranquillity* (London: Fisher Unwin, 1905), p. xii.

8. See Peter Brooks, *Reading for the Plot: Design and Intention in Narrative* (New York: Knopf, 1984).

9. Shakespeare, *Hamlet*, 3.1.65–66.

10. Mark Currie, *About Time: Narrative, Fiction and the Philosophy of Time* (Edinburgh: Edinburgh University Press, 2007), p. 107.

11. Paul Ricoeur *Time and Narrative*, vol. 2 (Chicago: University of Chicago Press, 1985), trans. Kathleen McLaughlin and David Pellauer, p. 108.

12. Marcel Proust, *Remembrance of Things Past* vol. 1 (London: Chatto and Windus, 1981), trans. C.K. Scott Moncrieff and Terence Kilmartin, p. 47.

13. William Faulkner, *Requiem for a Nun* (London: Chatto and Windus, 1965), p. 85.

14. Marcel Proust, *Remembrance of Things Past* vol. 3 (London: Chatto and Windus, 1981), trans. C.K. Scott Moncrieff and Terence Kilmartin, p. 1105.

15. Virginia Woolf, *To the Lighthouse* (London: Grafton, 1977), p. 151.

16. Samuel Beckett, *Proust, and Three Dialogues with Georges Duthuit* (London: Calder, 1965), p. 14.

17. DeLillo, *The Body Artist*, p. 67.

18. Virginia Woolf, *Mrs Dalloway* (London: Everyman, 1993), p. 46.

19. See Judith Halberstam, *In a Queer Time and Place: Transgender Bodies, Subcultural Lives* (New York: New York University Press, 2005).

20. The IPCC report is published in full at www.ipcc.ch/apps/eventma nager/documents/19/021120141253-Doc.%2021%20-%20Synthesis %20Report%20-%20Adopted%20Longer%20report.pdf.

21. Richard Powers, 'The Seventh Event', in *Granta*, vol. 90 (2005), p. 59.

5 THE NOVEL, JUSTICE AND THE LAW

1. Victor Hugo, *Les Misérables* (London: Penguin, 1982), trans. Norman Denny, p. 15.

2. Maurice Blanchot, *The Work of Fire* (Stanford: Stanford University Press, 1995), trans. Charlotte Mendell, p. 310.

3. Fyodor Dostoyevsky, *Crime and Punishment* (London: Penguin, 2003), trans. David McDuff, p. 312.

4. Ian McEwan, 'The Law Versus Religious Belief', in *The Guardian*, 5 September 2014, online at www.theguardian.com/books/2014/sep/ 05/ian-mcewan-law-versus-religious-belief.

5. Charlotte Perkins Gilman, *Herland*, in Charlotte Perkins Gilman, *The Yellow Wallpaper, Herland, and Selected Writings* (London: Penguin, 2009), p. 102.
6. Arthur Conan Doyle, *The Sign of Four*, in Arthur Conan Doyle, *The Complete Sherlock Holmes* (London: Penguin, 1981), p. 111.
7. Lukács, *The Meaning of Contemporary Realism*, p. 29.
8. Dostoyevsky, *Crime and Punishment*, p. 378.
9. Thomas More, *Utopia* (Cambridge: Cambridge University Press, 2002), p. 82.
10. Nathalie Babel Brown, *Hugo and Dostoevsky* (Ann Arbor: Ardis, 1978), p. 150.
11. Lukács, *The Meaning of Contemporary Realism*, p. 45.
12. Lukács, *The Meaning of Contemporary Realism*, p. 45.
13. Franz Kafka, *The Trial* (London: Penguin, 200), trans. Idris Parry, p. 2.
14. Coetzee, *Elizabeth Costello*, p. 19.
15. Shakespeare, *Hamlet*, 4.5.174.
16. Eliot, *Daniel Deronda*, p. 139.
17. Franz Kafka, *Diaries 1910–1923* (New York: Shocken Books, 1964), ed. Max Brod, p. 303.

CONCLUSION: THE THING WHICH IS NOT

1. Melville, *Moby Dick*, p. 277.
2. Will Self, 'The Novel is Dead (this time it's for real)', *The Guardian*, 2 May 2014, np. www.theguardian.com/books/2014/may/02/will-self-novel-dead-literary-fiction (last accessed 21 November 2014).
3. George Orwell, *Nineteen Eighty-Four* (London: Penguin, 1989), p. 29.
4. Samuel Beckett, *First Love*, in Beckett, *The Expelled and Other Novellas*, p. 10.
5. Swift, *Gulliver's Travels*, p. 236.

Index

Printed in the United States
By Bookmasters